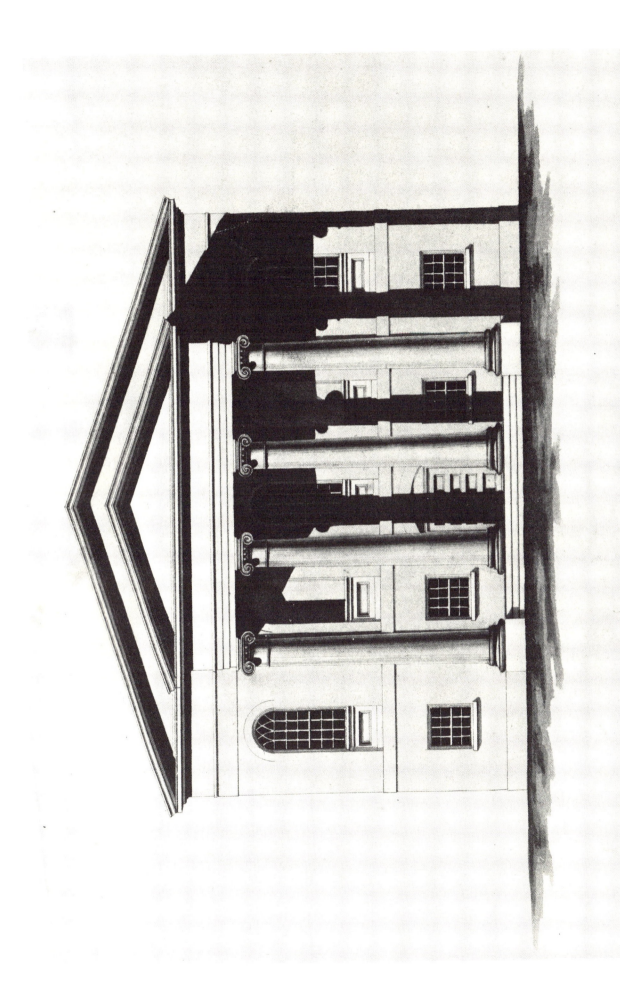

Elevation of the Kershaw Courthouse by Robert Mills, c. 1828.

ROBERT MILLS'S

COURTHOUSES & JAILS

by
Gene Waddell
and
Rhodri Windsor Liscombe

SOUTHERN HISTORICAL PRESS
EASLEY, SOUTH CAROLINA

SOUTHERN HISTORICAL PRESS
The Rev. Silas Emmett Lucas, Jr., Publisher
Post Office Box 738
Easley, South Carolina 29640

Library of Congress
Catalog card no. 81-86335
ISBN-0-89308-249-X

for

Philippa Windsor Liscombe

CONTENTS

ACKNOWLEDGEMENTS

Dr. Liscombe's research was sponsored by the Social Sciences and Humanities Research Council of Canada during the summer of 1980. Both authors are grateful for the research and editorial assistance provided by Philippa Windsor Liscombe. Several institutions cooperated to make available the information needed for this study and particularly the staffs of the South Carolina Department of Archives and History (hereafter SCDAH), the South Caroliniana Library (SCL), the South Carolina Historical Society (SCHS), and the Library of Congress (LC). Numerous individuals have also provided information and assistance, including Dr. Robert L. Alexander, Mrs. William P. Baldwin, Richard X. Evans, Mrs. Charles Gignilliat, Jr., Augustus T. Graydon, Harlan Greene, E.L. Inabinett, Dr. Charles H. Lesser, David Moltke-Hansen, C. Ford Peatross, Miss Elise Pinckney, Dr. George C. Rogers, Horace Fraser Rudisill, Miss Anna Wells Rutledge, E.D. Sloan, Jr., Michael Stauffer, and Dr. Allen Stokes.

SOURCES OF ILLUSTRATIONS

Abbeville County Museum: 56A.
Abby Aldrich Rockefeller Folk Art Center, Williamsburg, Virginia: 16.
Charleston Library Society: 51B.
Columbia University Press: 8A.
Darlington County Historical Commission: 32A.
Gibbes Art Gallery, Carolina Art Association: 44.
Historic American Buildings Survey: 26, 27, 28 (J. Whitney Cunningham and Ralph Little).
Historic Savannah Foundation: 1A, 1B (Frederick Spitzmiller).
Library of Congress: 29B, 37.
Lower Savannah Council of Governments: 57B (Ron McCall).
Manuscripts Department, University of Virginia Library: 24A.
National Archives and Records Service: 48, 49.
E.D. Sloan, Jr.: 17, 18A.
SCDAH: 2, 3, 4, 5, 6, 9, 10A, 11, 12, 13, 14, 15, 30C, 31, 32B, 33, 57A, 58B.
SCHS: Frontispiece, 10B, 19B, 23, 24B, 25A, 29A, 30B, 36B, 39, 40, 43A, 47, 53, 58A, 59.
SCL: 18B, 20, 22 (Carl Julien), 34, 38 (Stan Lewis), 45, 46, (Carl Julien), 52A (Stan Lewis),
    52B, 54 (Carl Julien), 55, 56B (Carl Julien), 58B.
Southeastern Architectural Archive, Tulane University Library: 7.
Valentine Museum (Cook Collection): 50.
Virginia State Library: 25B.
Gene Waddell: 8B, 21, 35B, 35C, 42, 43B.
WPA *History of Spartanburg County*: 36A.

LIST OF ILLUSTRATIONS

ROBERT MILLS'S COURTHOUSES AND JAILS

Robert Mills (1781-1855) returned to South Carolina in 1820 following two decades of professional training and practice in Washington, D.C., Philadelphia and Baltimore. Nine years later he moved back to Washington and eventually secured employment by the Federal Government. The period he spent in his native State, 1820-1829, coming at a midpoint in his career, was among Mills's most productive. However, the major group of works he executed for the State, approximately twenty-eight of the forty courthouses and jails erected during the decade, remain to be analyzed even though the sixteen courthouses he designed represent the largest body of his important public buildings.[1] The courthouses illuminate the development of his mature style, both in terms of his distinctive classical idiom and progressive planning and structural method. Furthermore, he established five new types for the courthouse (and two for the jail) and raised the standard of design and construction. In place of the customary and inconsequential wooden courthouse with a hipped roof, flank entrance, and ground floor courtroom, Mills popularized a brick building with a gable roof, raised and pedimented portico, and a courtroom elevated above vaulted, fireproof offices. No less an aesthetic and functional improvement were Mills's jails, which reflected his interest in penal reform. These precedents, apart from the sophisticated vaulting techniques, were closely followed in South Carolina throughout the nineteenth century. The study of Mills's contribution to judicial architecture in the State also provides a valuable commentary on public patronage in that era.

By 1820 Mills had become one of the few American architects with a national reputation. He had obtained the best training available in the United States, and he had already designed major buildings in six states.[2] Late in 1820 Mills quitted Baltimore because, as he wrote on 30 October, "the state of business in my profession have put it entirely out of my power to support my family."[3] Mills soon afterwards began his involvement in the scheme for internal improvements which had been initiated by the South Carolina Legislature in 1817, using excess

revenues accumulated in the prosperity following the cessation of the War of 1812 and the Napoleonic Wars.[4] On 20 December 1820 the South Carolina Legislature elected him to be one of the two paid members of its Board of Public Works. Given the title of "Acting Commissioner," he was primarily responsible for designing and supervising the erection of all state and district public buildings. Both the background to his election and the course of his official employment are complex and need to be summarized.

He inherited a situation in which several courthouses had been recently completed, begun, or designed under the authority of the Board of Public Works, which had been established in December 1819.[5] The five-man Board was headed by its two paid members, or Acting Commissioners, Abram Blanding and, at first, Thomas Baker, respectively responsible for the Departments of Roads, Rivers and Canals and of Public Buildings. This agency had replaced the office of Civil and Military Engineer.[6] Created in December 1817 to provide a co-ordinator for internal improvements throughout the State, the earlier post had been held by John Wilson.[7] Wilson was a professional engineer and surveyor, rather than an architect, and he had found the multifarious responsibilities of his office impossible for one person to manage. In order to regularize the architectural commissions, previously conducted under individual appropriations for each district building, the Board soon hired one of its non-paid members, the English architect William Jay (c. 1794-1837), to prepare six sets of drawings so that courthouses and jails could be erected to stock plans. This scheme, intended to reduce expenditure, was being implemented when the Board, in effect, employed Mills to replace both Baker and Jay. Mills was able to convince the Board that construction should be halted on all buildings that could be redesigned. Thus major revisions in Jay's plans occupied Mills during part of 1821, his first year on the Board, but he also prepared new designs in time for the Board to request funds from the Legislature at its end-of-the-year session in December. During his second year, 1822, he provided further new designs for approval by the Board.

Then, in December 1822, the Legislature abolished the Board and divided its authority between the two former Acting Commissioners. Blanding became Superintendent of Public Works,[8] and Mills Superintendent of Public Buildings. Mills's position was created for one year only, from December 1822 to December 1823. It was re-instated for another year, but occupied by Evander McIver, whose tenure also only lasted for a single year. While McIver was Superintendent, he frequently turned to Mills for designs.

Although Mills was primarily involved, from 1824 to 1828, in the preparation and then promotion of an atlas and volume of statistics of South Carolina, he also worked as an architect in private practice and continued to design most of the State's public buildings. After December 1824, when the office of Superintendent of Public Buildings was abolished, the local Commissioners often consulted Mills regarding designs, but in the second half of the 1820's, economic conditions progressively worsened, and by 1829 nearly all public construction had ceased. Mills returned to the North, after a sojourn at Abbeville[9], to supervise the erection of Enrico Causici's statue of Washington on the Monument in Baltimore, before moving soon thereafter to the District of Columbia in search of Federal employment.

Thus Mills's public work completed during his residence in South Carolina can be divided into four phases: his redesign of Jay's architecture (1821); his designs as Acting Commissioner that were subject to approval by the Board of Public Works (1821-1822); his independent designs as Superintendant of Public Buildings (1823); and his output for the State while he was in private practice (1824-1829). Based on original documentary material that is mainly preserved in the South Carolina Department of Archives and History, this study attributes the following courthouses to Mills (with surviving buildings indicated by an asterisk): Abbeville, Chesterfield, Colleton (redesigned by Mills), Darlington, Fairfield (redesigned by Mills and since altered)*, Georgetown,* Greenville, Horry,* Kershaw (since altered),* Marion, Marlborough, Newberry, Orangeburg, Union, Williamsburg (since altered),* and York. Relying upon the same sources, the following

jails are attributed to Mills: Charleston (separate wing), Colleton (redesigned by Mills), Edgefield, Greenville, Lancaster,* Laurens, Marion, Marlborough, Newberry, Spartanburg, Union,* Williamsburg, and, possibly, Horry and Orangeburg.

Mills and the Jay Buildings

William Jay had been elected a member of the Board of Public Works on 24 December 1819, and within about two weeks the Board had decided to dispense with plans previously adopted for courthouses needed for Fairfield, Sumter and Chester Districts.[10] On 9 February 1820 William H. Gibbes, Secretary to the Board, informed Baker that its members were "of the opinion that it would be best to construct all buildings upon the same plan." Gibbes had, therefore, written to Major Wilson requesting him to "get Mr. Jay to make out a Plan for a courthouse and gaol and forward it as soon as possible."[11]

A few days earlier, an advertisement had appeared in a Charleston newspaper inviting bids for four courthouses and four jails.[12] The courthouses were to be built for Sumter, Chester, Fairfield, and Marlborough Districts. The Sumter Courthouse was eventually built to Jay's plans, and the Chester courthouse was probably also; Fairfield's Courthouse was begun using Jay's plans, but, as will be shown, was redesigned by Mills; the construction of the Marlborough Courthouse was delayed, and Jay's plans were not used. The Colleton Courthouse and Jail had been authorized earlier and were soon begun to Jay's plans, but were also redesigned by Mills. The Beaufort Courthouse was already under construction and was being built to similar designs that are attributable to Jay. (Figures 2-3). The four jails mentioned in the advertisement were for Chester, Marlborough, Abbeville, and Pendleton. The Pendleton Jail was eventually completed to Jay's plans (Figures 12-13) and alone survives of his South Carolina public buildings; Marlborough was delayed, and his plans were not used; the Chester Jail was probably completed to Jay's plans, but with minor alterations by Mills; the existing Abbeville Jail was repaired and not replaced for several decades. One set of Jay's jail plans may have been adapted for the Sumter Jail (Figures 14-15).[13]

2

Construction must have been delayed on all these buildings while Jay prepared his new stock plans and made six copies of the drawings (compare Figures 4-5 and 12-13) and specifications. Not until 12 May was he paid for this work, and six days later, the specifications for the Colleton Courthouse and Jail were accepted by its contractor (Appendix II, 1).[14] At the end of 1820, Baker reported that "agreeable to the directions of the Board, I obtained from the architect appointed by them, drafts for the Court House and Gaol, according to a uniform plan, and formed the contracts with reference to them."

The preoccupation with a uniform design was presumably to provide each district with an equally respectable courthouse that could be built for a predictable sum. While politically expedient and administratably reasonable, the objective was not architecturally sound since it ignored the differences in space needed for courtrooms and offices and in site, materials, and craftsmen. In some areas clay suitable for the manufacture of bricks was unavailable; in others there were no qualified masons available because of the great amount of work being undertaken on canals and roads in South Carolina and elsewhere. Naturally the scheme was also disadvantageous to architects because it diminished their opportunities for employment.

When Mills joined the Board in December 1820 he judged Jay's courthouse plan to be inconveniently arranged and deficient in not being fireproof.[15] In the section on "District Public Buildings" in the 1821 report of the Board, not signed but attributable to him, Mills recommended that construction be stopped pending redesign.[16] As building had, in any case, not progressed very far, he revised the courthouses for Colleton and Fairfield as completely as he could, repositioning the courtroom on the second floor. In this process he created another standard design, which he, nonetheless, abandoned when devising a new plan for the as yet unbuilt Marlborough Courthouse. A drawing of the Colleton Courthouse as completed (Figure 6), when compared with Jay's specifications, shows that Mills reversed the relative heights of the two stories so that the first was much lower than the second; he placed the courtroom above the offices, thereby obviating a

frequent complaint in grand jury presentments that the court was exposed to noise from the adjacent streets.[17] When Mills assumed control, the walls had been partly raised and the first-floor joints inserted. The contractor advised the retention of these joints while changing the internal layout, as Mills desired without any increase in the contract price.[18] Consequently the ground floor was neither vaulted nor made fireproof, though it was fronted by a single-storied, Tuscan portico. A contemporary drawing of the Fairfield public buildings shows a courthouse almost identical with the one in the drawings of Colleton, excepting the omission of a portico (Figure 7).[19] The original Fairfield building survives, sandwiched between a later, two-storied portico at the front and a rear extension. As with Colleton, the Fairfield interior was without the vaulting.

Mills's intentions were further expressed in his 1821 report. A preceding attitude on the part of the Legislature that favored "false economy, calculating alone the minimum of expenditures, without regarding the permanency of the object" had resulted in the poor condition of the existing courthouses. The majority had been built within the last twenty years, but with "bad materials and workmanship." Appropriations had been inadequate for both building and maintenance.[20] In addition, further damage was attributable to the absence of gutters to carry rain water beyond the foundations and of enclosures for protection against vandalism and to the exposure of the courtrooms to damage because stairs in them provided access to the offices above, and the courtrooms were even used as local meeting halls.[21] The jails were similarly insecure because of their faulty construction and lack of repair and because the jailers refused to occupy their quarters. Apart from his complaints about inadequate funding, Mills castigated the current system of making contracts, and he proposed the adoption of the practice common "in several of our Northern cities" of hiring a disinterested "mechanic" to obtain separate agreements for each trade, instead of leaving that responsibility with the individual contractors. His advocacy was successful, for the Board accepted the necessity of "a change in the present system of contracts . . . in order to secure to the state faithfulness in the execution of the buildings and economy in the expenditure of money" and persuaded the Legislature that "there is no fact in political economy more obvious than this, that money laid out in the execution of *temporary works* for *public purposes* is so much loss to the state."

During 1821, in addition to redesigning Jay's buildings and producing another prototype for Marlborough, Mills found time to prepare new courthouse designs for Greenville, Newberry, Williamsburg and York Districts, and new jail designs for Charleston, Lancaster, Spartanburg and Union. He also conceived designs for three major State buildings: the Fireproof Building, Charleston; the Lunatic Asylum, Columbia; and a group of nine powder magazines, near Charleston.

Mills as Acting Commissioner

Up to the time of his new appointment, work on the Marlborough Courthouse and Jail had stalled because all the bids were "several thousand dollars" above the appropriation, despite the fact that both were upon the plans "proposed to be generally adopted."[22] Therefore, Mills was free to submit new designs, the design for the courthouse becoming his most frequently used type, and the one for the jail seems to have also. He described the Marlborough buildings in his *Statistics of South Carolina*, published in 1826:

> In 1821-1822, a handsome court-house and jail were erected here of brick, rough-cast, to imitate stone-work. The offices under the courtroom are all vaulted, and made fireproof; all the rooms in the jail are also made indestructible by fire.
>
> The court-house presents, in front, a portico of Doric columns, surmounted by a pediment, raised on an arcade one story high. To the platform of the portico you ascend by a double flight of circular steps, from which you pass through a vestibule previous to entering the court room. On each side of the vestibule are two jury rooms, which open into the court room only, over which are the galleries.
>
> The jail presents a neat, characteristic front.[23]

This passage reflects Mills's conviction that jails should be secure but humane. One of his earliest major designs had been for the unexecuted South Carolina Penitentiary, 1806, and he wrote extensively on penal reform in his *Statistics*. Secure jails rendered "chaining, handcuffing, &c" unnecessary.[24] Moreover, he felt that jails should be as "indestructible by fire" as offices designed to protect public records. Earlier jails had been less secure, and they were bereft of adequate circulation of air and of separate accommodation for debtors (who had to be incarcerated with felons, some accused of violent crimes) and even for male and female prisoners. Mills was seeking to institute the more enlightened principles of the penitentiary such as those promoted by B.H. Latrobe and John Haviland, so that the State jail system could encourage rehabilitation during imprisonment.

In December 1821 the Legislature authorized appropriations for the large group of courthouses and jails that had been recommended by the Board. The variety of designs indicates that the Board was already using more than one set. For Greenville (Figure 16), Newberry, and York (Figure 18B), Mills adapted the Marlborough Courthouse plan with its raised, attached portico, again combining an essentially classical form with a Renaissance (and Colonial) facade composition.[25] York was constructed of stone and given a larger and distinctive courtroom, described in the *Statistics* as "spacious, convenient, and airy; amphitheatrical in its form, with a segment spherical ceiling."[26] The usual gallery extended over the jury rooms, which were situated on either side of the entrance to the court. At Williamsburg he chose the temple form with six columns resting on an arcaded base (Figure 22). Though twice renovated, its original plan remains intact. It differed in two respects from any other courthouse known to have been designed by Mills: the vaulting was purely segmental (not cross-vaulted as at Horry and other subsequent courthouses), which simplified the placing of the ground floor rooms (so that two lay to one side of the central hall and three to the other); and the external stairs were concealed behind the arcaded ground floor instead of flanking the portico as at most of his other courthouses.

The Union and Spartanburg Jails were

nearly identical, having an almost domestic appearance with hipped roofs and resembling Jay's courthouses and jails, while the details were distinctly Latrobian (Figures 34, 35 B-C, 36, and 37. Though similar in size, Mills decided upon a gable-ended composition for Lancaster that achieved a more monumental effect (Figure 38).[27] The exteriors of these two types of jails differ considerably, but the interiors have much the same plan with rooms on either side of a central hall, as on the lower floors of his courthouses.[28]

Mills as Superintendent of Public Buildings

In December 1822 when the Legislature determined the appropriations for the ensuing year, the construction and repair program was so extensive that funds only permitted the commissioning of two new courthouses, those for Georgetown and Marion. As early as 21 May 1822 W.J. Middleton, an employee of the Board of Works, warned Mills that the State fund "for Internal Improvement is very low."[29] And, by 1823, South Carolinians and their legislators had become, understandably, disillusioned with public works. The reasons lay less with the expenditure on public buildings than with the huge costs of the transportation network. Most of the one million dollars disbursed on roads and canals over the previous four years had produced meagre results; both systems were incomplete and thus partly or totally unusable. Compounding the problem was the division in executive powers, resulting in the incompetent supervision of contracts and budgets, besides the scarcity of skilled labor owing to the number of projects under way. To continue work in progress, a legislative committee recommended that the Board of Public Works be abolished and that its functions be divided between a Superintendent of Public Works and a Superintendent of Public Buildings, the two having "no connection."[30] Mills was appointed to the latter post, but, in the prevailing economic and political circumstances, he could not fully exercise his talents as an architect.

Before he assumed this new post, Mills defended the architectural policy of the Board in its final report and further recorded the reforms he had instituted during the previous two years:

The Board directed the plans of the building to be carefully made out with full drawings of every part there of, and a detailed specification of all the work, leaving the prices blank. They advertised for proposals from mechanicks, and before any contract was made — ascertained by requiring the blanks to be filled, the lowest price for which the work was offered to be done and closed their contracts accordingly.

They let it be distinctively understood that no proposals for work would be received from any but mechanics.

It may be proper here to observe that in the contracts made in the two last years for Goals and Court Houses — although the plans provide for all of them being made fireproof, and having larger accommodations than those constructed in 1819 and 1820 which were not fireproof — there has been a reduction of expense exceeding eleven percent on the prices paid for the later buildings.[31]

In 1823, as Superintendent of Public Buildings, Mills began the Georgetown and Marion Courthouses and prepared designs for three other courthouses and for two jails in time for them to be submitted for appropriations at the end of the year. In addition he was supervising the construction of courthouses for Chester, Greenville, Marlborough, Newberry and York; the jails for Lancaster, Spartanburg and Union; and the public buildings at Charleston and Columbia.[32] Judging by its lower appropriation, $10,000 as against $12,000, the Marion Courthouse, since demolished (the plans and specifications are also lost), probably did not copy his surviving Georgetown design, the most sophisticated of his South Carolina courthouses. The Georgetown facade is similar to that for Williamsburg, but has a more subtle decorative pattern and practical arrangement of entrances and stairs (Figure 23). The stairs are screened behind the channelled, rusticated basement and reached through the arched entrances to either side of the more richly ornamented office doorway, which is projected from rather than recessed behind the piers supporting the six Tuscan columns of its portico. As well as lending variety to the wall plane, the composition establishes a central emphasis, reinforced by the large doorway to the courtroom, without disturbing the symmetry of the templar format, and also the functional division of the two parts of the building. Acknowledging the desire for economy, Mills reverted to the Marlborough type in the three plans he submitted to the Legislature in December 1823 for Darlington, Horry and Union (Figures 32A, 21, and 20). The appropriations, $10,000 for each of these, and $8,000 each for new jails for Marion and Williamsburg, were approved (Appendix II, 3). Yet Mills found himself unaccountably replaced by McIver, who, during his year of tenure, largely supervised the construction of buildings designed and funded prior to the beginning of the year.[33]

Mills's Horry Courthouse stands relatively unchanged and typifies the appearance of the majority of those erected to his plans (Figure 21). The gabled main block is fronted by a tetrastyle portico elevated on an arcaded basement. However, Mills or possibly the contractor, Russell Warren, here tried yet another stair pattern, consisting of two flights of steps rising at right angles on each side of the portico (Appendix II, 4). As a counterpoint to the centralizing effect of the arched entrances to the offices below and courtroom above, Mills inserted niches at the upper level of the front hall. Unusual are the unfluted Greek Doric Order and the exposed brick walls which at the sides, nonetheless, have his preferred recession of the center bay with a triple window, which he also adopted on the Fireproof Building and Kershaw Courthouse (Figures 27 and 41).

The support for public improvements continued to decline throughout the year and, in December 1824, the Legislature did away with the office of Superintendent of Public Buildings. The mood of retrenchment influenced the inclusion in the appropriation bill of the stipulation that no public official could enter into any agreement in excess of the appropriation, at the peril of legal proceedings. Henceforth, a signed contract for the total amount of work envisaged must be on file with one of the State's two Treasurers before any payment would be made, and then only on the basis of a one third advance (with proper bond), a further third when half completed, and the remainder upon being received.[34] This legislation implies that contractors had not been held to the estimates in their original agreements which, as the financial records indicate, were usually exceeded. The contractors were not always to blame since the quantity of improvements both inside and outside the State had created scarcities in supplies as well as labor which caused steep rises in costs beyond those anticipated in the original contracts. Moreover, changes had often been ordered by the local commissioners (not infrequently without the authority of a State agency) or by the contractor during construction. In an unusual case, Mills himself stipulated that stone had to be substituted for the walls of the Union Jail because the brick had proved to be unsatisfactory through no fault of the supplier. Because of such changes, the December 1824 appropriations bill included "extra" payments to the contractors of the courthouses for Chester, Greenville, and York Districts. Meanwhile, and unfortunately for Mills, the expenditures on the Fireproof Building and the Asylum were continuing to mount alarmingly. Undoubtedly inflation was the major reason, but Mills often suffered criticism for the overruns. Still, his work was vigorously defended. An anonymous Charlestonian asserted that he had saved the State over $30,000 by designing superior buildings costing 20 per cent less than those of his predecessors and that he had been replaced "without the shadow of any imputation against him."[35] The financial records support this claim, and Mills's services as an architect continued to be utilized by the State.

For his own part Mills attributed his dismissal entirely to the political opposition to public works inside South Carolina; writing to Robert Gilmor from Columbia on 2 September 1824, he stated:

> You no doubt have long known how the Legislature of my native state served me — First by the intrigue of a few who were enemies to internal improvement in the state. These individuals gathered

6

strength, and induced their colleagues to abolish the Board of public work altogether. Thus was I thrown suddenly out of employment, — out of the means of support and in a place where but little call for the exercise of my profession existed . . . . I could not have expected such treatment as I rec'd from the Legislature of my own state, but the imprudent expenditures on the internal improvement system of this state previous to my coming into office occasioned the abolishment of the office, and I believe that if they could have done it the whole system would have been also abandoned — Tho' I was able to economise in the public works during my time to the amt. 30 thousand dollars — This was but a drop in the bucket.[36]

Over the next two years, Mills was to find some consolation in the compilation and then publication of his *Atlas* and the associated volume of *Statistics*.[37]

Mills in Private Practice

On 8 December 1824 the House and Senate both tersely "resolved, That it is inexpedient to re-establish the office of superintendent of public buildings." Yet many districts required new courthouses and jails; and the local commissioners, now charged with the responsibility of commissioning designs, not unnaturally tended to engage Mills. The needs of Kershaw District, for instance, could not be long neglected since its courthouse was in a deplorable condition and was situated in Camden, one of the major towns of the State. Thus the Legislature authorized a courthouse for Kershaw, another for Chesterfield, and a new jail for Horry. Mills's authorship of the design for the Kershaw Courthouse is unusually well documented; there are extant the official receipt for the plans and a bond and an agreement stating that these were to be implemented (Appendix II, 7). It is also the only courthouse for which an original drawing of his has been preserved (Frontispiece), though it probably dates from about 1828 and seems to illustrate either a penultimate stage in the

design or a subsequent revision; whichever applies, the design monumentalizes his main courthouse type of a pedimented portico projected from a gable-ended temple form building. The Chesterfield Courthouse can also be attributed to him because its specifications required that his plans were to be adopted with minor changes (Appendix II, 6A). The Horry Jail, for which minimal records remain, was probably by him, not least since it was begun in the same month that the courthouse was finished to his design. Obviously he was still functioning as the State's architect, even though he had occupied no government position during the previous year.

Mills judged the Kershaw Courthouse to be his finest, up to 1826; he wrote in the *Statistics* that it was "superior in its design to any in the state both for convenience of accommodation, beauty, and permanency." And he went on to justify his opinion by describing the building at some length:

> Its facade presents a grand portico of six Ionic columns,[38] spreading the whole extent of the building, and rising so high that the main roof will cover it, and constitute its pediment. The offices (six in number) occupy the lower or basement story, arched with brick, and made fire-proof: a double flight of stairs rises within the vestibule to the court-room story, which occupies the most of the second floor: the jury-rooms on this floor are so disposed as to admit the galleries to extend over them. Four columns rise in this court-room, carrying their imposts, between which springs a grand arched ceiling, the whole width of the room, and extending its entire length.
>
> Including the portico, the building is 62 feet long, and 43 feet wide. The roof is proposed to be covered with metal, copper or zinc,) so that a permanency and security from fire will be given to the whole edifice; the walls are of brick.

Mills's preference for this building may owe to its grander scale and purer external form. But in one respect the design was inferior to his earlier courthouses, for the location of the main stairs on the interior robbed the courtroom of space; these were later removed. When he came to plan the courthouse for Alexandria, Virginia, in 1838, he reverted to his former composition of two flights of steps flanking the portico, and placed a smaller staircase inside (Figures 48-49). A fair comparison of the aesthetic merits of the Kershaw Courthouse with its preceding types is impossible because the building was substantially altered in 1845, including the substitution of a tetrastyle Greek Doric portico pierced by an ungainly central staircase (Figures 25A and 26-28).

Equally distinctive was Mills's 1825 design for the Chesterfield Courthouse (Figure 29). The specifications state that he was to be paid $25 for his "drafts," since lost, and that the local commissioners had "adopted the plan furnished by Robert Mills, with a few alterations" (Appendix II, 6). Chief among the differences were its three stories and the entrances placed on a broader side. The first story had two cross-vaulted rooms on each side of a barrel-vaulted hall, the second a courtroom entered through an attached portico raised on an arcaded basement, and the third four jury rooms reached by two flights of internal stairs.[39] The specifications provide important details about the reinforcement Mills planned for the vaulting, details that merit repeating here:

> The first story to commence two feet thick, and to be secured by interties of iron of the following description (To Wit) six bars, one and one fourth inch Square, to extend across the building under the court room floor, headed at each end with axe bar iron eighteen inches in length five d[itto]. crossing length ways in the same manner, all of which are to be concealed within the work.[40]

The walls were "to be laid in good strong lime mortar solid through." With the reinforcement Mills stipulated, the valuting would have been as secure against structural defects as was then feasible.

Probably in 1825, Mills also designed a courthouse and jail for Orangeburg (Figure 19B); both were begun the following year. The courthouse conformed with his main type (begun at Marlborough). To these may be added the Newberry Jail, commenced in 1826 and again suggesting that Mills had presented a plan to the Legislature for approval before December 1825; the specifications required it to be similar to the Edgefield Jail, the specifications for which noted that it was to be identical with the Union Jail.

After 1825 Mills continued to be chosen to design many, but not all, of the district buildings, and he probably designed Charleston's Citadel.[41] A number of courthouses and jails, though designed by others, were essentially copies of his work (as in Figure 30C). His virtual monopoly ended in 1826; the Lancaster Courthouse, begun in that year, while reflecting the influence of Chesterfield in its side portico, has Georgian style features uncharacteristic of his current architecture (Figure 52A).[42] Nevertheless, in 1826 he probably designed the jail for Laurens that was to be like the one at Union. His continued involvement in the district building program is reflected in a further letter to Gilmor, written from Columbia on 26th May 1826; Mills wrote he had "just returned home after an absence of upwards of two months in the low country where I have been constantly occupied in looking after the public buildings executing in that part of the State."[43] The next year he may have supplied drawings and specifications for the similarly planned Greenville Jail. Again writing to Gilmor from Columbia, on 13 March (1827), he mused on the prospect: "I shall soon be idle, this I cannot afford, and even if I could it is not in my disposition to desire it."

The construction of public buildings decreased sharply after 1827. Economic conditions had deteriorated to the point that in December 1828 the Legislature passed a resolution requesting that the Controller General inquire into the expediency of a general reduction in the public expenditures and taxation. A tax cut was enacted in 1829, the year that Mills returned to Baltimore (in October) to complete the Washington Monument. But from at least as early as 1826, he had been applying for a position with the

Federal Government; and in 1827 he wrote to a friend that he was:

> tired of wandering about from state to state dependent upon the precarious business created by the act of Legislative bodies. You know I have been engaged for the past six or seven years in the work of Internal Improvements in this state — This work is now brought nearly to a close, and my professional engagements with it — I have felt desirous to enter into the service of the general government even at a moderate salary rather than run the risk of getting a large salary from the state governments, as I believe there would be more stability in the office under the former.
>
> I shall have to leave this state soon, as there is now no field for the exercise of my profession.[44]

The Design Types and Sources of Mills's Courthouses and Jails

Mills's courthouses can be divided into five basic types: (1) A gable-ended building with a ground floor entrance on one of its longer sides (the redesigned Jay courthouses for Colleton and Fairfield; Figures 6-7); (2) A gable-ended building with an attached tetrastyle portico raised on an arcaded basement and placed on one of its shorter sides (Abbeville, Darlington, Greenville, Horry, Marlborough, Newberry, Orangeburg, Union and York; Figures 32A, 16, 21, 19B, 20, and 18B); (3) A temple form building spanned by a hexastyle portico elevated on an arcaded basement (Georgetown and Williamsburg; Figures 22 and 23); (4) A three story building with a gabled roof and a raised, attached portico on one of its longer sides (Chesterfield; Figure 29A); and (5) A temple form building fronted by a monumental portico (Kershaw; Frontispiece). Each, excepting Chesterfield, had two stories with the courtroom on the second floor reached by exterior stairs, apart from the revised Jay type and Kershaw Courthouse. The majority have porticoes of the Tuscan Order, the exceptions being for Horry (unfluted Greek Doric) and Kershaw (Ionic). Of particular interest is Mills's limited use of the pure temple form,

despite its appropriate symbolism and increasing popularity in contemporary American architecture, including the courthouses erected during this period in Virginia under the influence of Jefferson.[45] Indeed, Mills only adopted it for the more populous districts of Georgetown, Kershaw, and Williamsburg.[46]

The basic requirements that Mills had to satisfy were similar to those for local courthouses and jails elsewhere in the United States during the first half of the nineteenth century. The two primary functions of the courthouses were judicial and administrative, respectively calling for a court and jury rooms and an office for the Clerk of Court, whose duties necessitated the provision of one or more rooms for various kinds of public records.[47] A few districts had separate registers of mesne conveyance, and the sheriff had an office in the courthouse rather than the jail. A meeting room for local commissions (concerning buildings, roads, etc.) is occasionally mentioned in the documents. These rooms were essentially undifferentiated, and Mills designated all rooms on the ground floors of his courthouses as "offices." Thus his principal considerations in designing his courthouses were fireproof storage for public records and a courtroom of adequate size, having convenient but controlled access. His invariable solution of placing the offices on the ground floor, with the courtroom above, yielded considerable functional improvements over Jay's scheme and the traditional single-storied courthouse of Virginia.[48] This arrangement also made possible the limitation of the fireproofing to the lower floor; the courtroom of the Williamsburg courthouse, for example, burned in 1883 without harm to records stored beneath. Mills provided for the fireproofing requirements through the use of masonry vaulting (Figure 42).

Another significant factor in the design process should be addressed before embarking upon an analysis of the courthouse types Mills developed. In no known instance was he able to select their sites (or of his jails), nor is there any record of his having specified a preference for their orientation. Generally, the site of the former courthouse was reused, or the Legislature authorized the local commissioners to select one. So most of his buildings stood on or faced the public squares, where, a statute of 1809 stated, the "gaols and courthouses in the several districts are erected." At Darlington, its courthouse occupied a position on one corner that was directly opposite another square, while at Newberry, one was set back thirty-seven feet from the street, but conventionally centered near one end of a two clock square (Figures 31E and 30A). Of his four surviving courthouses originally having porticoes, the one for Williamsburg faces north, those for Georgetown and Horry northeast, and for Kershaw east.[49]

Having arrived at a basic solution for the plan of his courthouses, Mills continued to experiment with alternative compositions for the access to the courtroom — and thus of the facade — apparently never being entirely satisfied with any. First, for Marlborough, he placed the stairs on either side of the basement of the attached portico so as to free the entrance to the central, ground floor hall (as for Union; Figure 20). Next, for Williamsburg, the portico rested on a basement having a single arch leading to the offices. The stairs are both concealed behind the flanking blind arcades. But, while the entrance to the courtroom was visible on the upper story, the access to the stairs was not evident (Figure 22). Then, for Georgetown, he sought to achieve a better aesthetic balance and more direct functional expression by again spanning the courtroom with a full portico elevated on a basement, but now pierced by three openings respectively giving entry to the ground floor (at the center) and stairs (Figure 23). Despite its architectural distinction, he reverted to his initial solution for most of his other courthouses, the major exception being Kershaw (Frontispiece) and minor exceptions being the L-shaped stairs of Horry and Darlington (Figures 21 and 32A). Economic considerations do not seem to have been the principal reason for the predominance of the Marlborough type since he adapted its portico and stairs arrangement for his much more costly Fireproof Building and Asylum (Figures 39-41 and 43B). He only abandoned the attempt to express dual functions for Kershaw, probably because he decided to cover the front with a monumental portico.[50]

Both the full temple form and Mills's preceding design types only allowed for ex-

pansion at the rear. Within thirty years many of the courthouses did have their courtrooms and office space enlarged by the removal of the jury rooms from the entrance end (where the deliberations of the juries could often be overheard) to an upstairs section behind the judge's bench; the corresponding space created below was utilized for administration (as in Figures 9, 28, and 33). Apart from those for Georgetown and Williamsburg, his relatively narrow courtrooms were eventually either replaced or adapted to other uses. Nor was the amphitheatral plan for his York Courthouse sufficiently large to meet the increasing demands of legal administration after the War Between the States, as was true of Jay's courthouses. Mills's plan, rather than resembling Jay's, may have been related to the oval courtroom he had envisaged in his unexecuted design for the Richmond City Hall and Courthouse, 1816 (Figure 29B).[51]

The fundamental influence on Mills's temple form courthouses was the Palladian tradition, both as exemplified in Colonial South Carolina architecture and in the original designs of Palladio which he had early studied in the library of Thomas Jefferson, who greatly admired the work of the sixteenth century Italian architect. From Jefferson, rather than Latrobe or the contemporary Greek Revival, Mills seems to have derived the full portico, whether raised on a basement or freestanding. The fenestration and recessed panels on most of his courthouses, however, issued from Latrobe (and, to a lesser extent, from Charles Bulfinch), who had also taught him advanced vaulting techniques. Mills re-interpreted his sources to create novel designs appropriate to South Carolina.

The breadth of Mills's synthesis of sources is epitomized by the motif he employed most frequently: a pedimented portico raised on an arcaded basement. Popularized in the United States through the publications of Palladio and his followers, numerous variations existed in his native Charleston. In his *Statistics* Mills praised the one most suited to his judicial architecture: the Charleston District "court-house (formerly the state house) is another of those substantial and well arranged buildings which do credit to the art. The principal front . . . presents a central projection, formed by a screen of [engaged] columns raised on a rustic arcade, the whole rising the entire height of the building . . ." (Figure 51A).[52] He also lauded the Exchange as a building whose appearance "proves that the hand of science was engaged in its design," which embraced the same motif and a basement with groin vaulting.[53]

Mills owned a "French edition" of Scamozzi's celebrated work on Palladio, and although he denied ever consulting books when designing a building, he may well have looked carefully at the elevation of the Villa Arsiero, Vicenza (Figure 19A).[54] This has a raised portico elevated on an arcaded basement and the fenestration is similar despite the different number of stories. Charles Bulfinch, to whom Jefferson had written a letter of introduction for the young Mills on 1 July 1802, had fashioned a double portico effect, notwithstanding the insertion of the base of a steeple, for the facade of his Congregational Church at Taunton, Massachusetts, 1790-1792.[55]

The most direct source for the dual entrances and curved stairs was probably Charleston City Hall (Figure 50), built circa 1800 as a branch of the Bank of the United States and almost certainly designed by the amateur architect, Gabriel Manigault. Although Mills professed to dislike the building, he echoed its siting and massing, and probably also the stairs, when designing his neighboring Fireproof Building. The curving stairs that were probably added to the tetrastyle portico of the South Carolina State House in 1811 provided another model.[56] The offices in the State House at Columbia were situated on the ground floor, as Mills noted in his *Statistics*, wherein he also described it as "neat in its general appearance and commodious" (Figure 51B).[57] And again, it is worthy of note that Bulfinch seems to have elevated the courtroom in his Worcester County Courthouse at Worcester, Massachusetts, 1801-1803, above office accommodation.[58]

The pure temple form, particularly when raised on a full ground floor, doubtless derives from Jefferson's Virginia Capitol, 1785-1789 (Figure 25B); Jefferson's influence on Mills revived during the 1820s. The Capitol had been built without stairs across the front, instead having a single entrance beneath the portico, features not in Jefferson's original designs but, nonetheless, ones that render the building a probable source for the George-

town and Williamsburg Courthouses. Pavilion VII at the University of Virginia (Figure 24A), founded on an 1817 design by William Thornton, has a temple-form building with a hexastyle portico on an arcaded basement that compares, in its composition and proportions, with those two courthouses, but the concept is not so unusual as to rule out coincidence.[59] The full length columns of Kershaw could have been inspired by Pavilion V as well as the Virginia Capitol, or by Latrobe's Bank of Pennsylvania, 1799-1800, of which Mills had made a drawing in about 1803 (now on exhibition at Monticello).

Mill's most obvious examples for vaulting were Latrobe's Washington Federal commissions (in the summer of 1804 he was assisting Latrobe at the Capitol), and also the relevant sections in Palladio's *Four Books*. And he would have known of the vaults used in Charleston, including those on the ground floor of the Exchange, the tower of St. Michael's Church, and the Powder Magazine on Cumberland Street, all of which were within a few blocks of his residence as a youth.[60] He had put these techniques into practice on the fireproof wings he erected alongside the Pennsylvania State House (Independence Hall), Philadelphia, 1812; and he unsuccessfully proposed that his Washington Hall, built in that city 1809-1816, be vaulted (it burned in 1823).

In designing for his courthouses, Mills consistently introduced classical allusions, compositional more than ornamental, to designate their status and to dignify their social functions. Given their radically different purpose, he avoided classical allusions in his jails; indeed their combination of small openings set into thick walls has an almost medieval cast. That is heightened at Union by the stone facing, if counteracted by the triple-arched porch, possibly derived from engravings of Palladio's Villa Saraceno (Figure 34 and 35A).[61] The plain surfaces and neatly handled openings look back via his own prison at Burlington, New Jersey, designed 1808 (but with an E shaped plan), to Latrobe's designs for the Richmond Penitentiary, 1797-1798, and Allegheny Arsenal, 1814 (Figure 37). And as utilitarian buildings, Mills's jails more closely resembled the nineteenth and twentieth century functionalist traditions than did his courthouses for his South Carolina jails substantiated his claim that, "Utility and economy will be found to have entered into most of the studies of the author, and little sacrificed to display; at the same time his endeavors were to produce as much harmony and beauty of arrangement as practicable."[62]

Nearest in design to his courthouses was the Lancaster Jail, a gable-ended building having its entrance centered on a shorter side (Figure 38). His other and predominant jail type, represented by Union (Figure 34), followed Jay's Pendleton Jail (Figure 12) in its domestic character — both have been converted to houses, Union into the Sheriff's residence — apart from the sophistication of its Latrobian recessed opening. Probably based on the Marlborough Jail, Union was copied at Edgefield, Greenville, Laurens and Newberry. The four-story addition he built adjacent to the Charleston Jail was of a different caliber, being designed for long-term and solitary confinement. The district jails correspond more with earlier than later South Carolina jails than do his courthouses. Brick or stone was employed for all jails known to have been built between 1800 and 1860, with one early and one late exception. The preceding jails were somewhat smaller, and the succeeding ones about half again larger than those by Mills. His contribution was to introduce aesthetic distinction and more humane and practical planning into an utilitarian building. Despite how well designed his jails were, though, no subsequent building is known to have been designed in imitation of either of the two basic types.

Mills usually ordered stone foundations, brick for the walls and partitions, and wood for the floors and ceilings. Lancaster alone is established as having vaulted interior spaces, comprising segmental unitary vaults, like those of the Williamsburg Courthouse, rather than his more prevalent segmental cross-vaults. However, his Marlborough Jail seems to have been vaulted, since it was fireproof, and others of his jails may have been similarly protected. The accommodation was undifferentiated aside from the provision of fireplaces in the jailer's quarters and debtor's room on the lower storey. Dangerous criminals were generally confined above, where escape and communication with the outside were more difficult.

The Context and Architectural Influence of Mills's Courthouses and Jails

Mills's designs for courthouses and jails, coming almost at the mid-point of his professional career, relate to his other designs of the 1820's and anticipate his subsequent work. The relationship with his earlier compositions is less pronounced, partly because these had mainly comprised domestic and religious commissions, and partly because he had then been influenced more by Latrobian than Palladian ideals. The major exception is his Burlington Prison, which had masonry vaulted cells, commodious quarters for the jailer and debtors, and a severe but finely proportioned facade. He rarely selected the temple form before 1820, beside his unexecuted scheme for an Episcopal church on John's Island, near Charleston, dating from late 1803 or early 1804. His Congregational, or Circular, Church, Charleston, 1804-1806, and Sansom Street, or Dr. Staughton's, Baptist Church, 1811-1812, and Unitarian, or Octagon, Church, 1811-1813, both in Philadelphia, the Monumental Church, Richmond, 1812-1814, and First Baptist Church, Baltimore, 1816-1818 — each with innovative central plans — had attached porticoes, but in each case the columns rested at or near ground level. While he spurned the conventional form for those churches, he echoed the traditional gable-ended main facade with attached portico in his courthouses. Lastly, his Washington Hall, Philadelphia, prefigured the courthouses in having the main accommodation on the upper floor and an elevated (*in antis*) portico.

He created a comparable re-interpretation of Colonial and Palladian themes in the major public commissions he undertook contemporaneously with the courthouses. Thus the most important, the Fireproof Building, Charleston, 1822-1826, and the Insane Asylum, Columbia, 1822-1827, were graced with attached porticoes, if of a more monumental scale, raised on full ground floors, flanking curved stairs and unobstructed entrances (Figures 39-40 and 43B).[63] Both also have masonry vaulted rooms. A similar portico composition, with an arcaded basement and originally, it would appear, curving stairs also occur on the house he designed for Ainsley Hall, built at Columbia, 1820-1823 (Figures 46 and 47A). The similarly designed

12

Columbia Academy could be attributed to him on stylistic grounds (Figure 45).[64] Mills employed the fully developed temple form for the Bethesda Presbyterian Church he had earlier completed in Camden, circa 1821-1822 (Figure 44), albeit raised on a Roman base akin to the original model prepared for the Virginia Capitol.[65] In company with the Fireproof Building, this church has pairs of entrances on the same level to facilitate access, a solution he could not have followed for both floors of the courthouses. His other principal public commission during the 1820's was for a group of nine powder magazines erected on Charleston Neck. These were constructed with domical vaults, apart from the larger, central magazine which had a circular vault with a central pier.[66]

Mills continually experimented with the raised attached portico motif, reverting to it in a series of unexecuted designs, a number being sketched into his 1837-1840 notebook, including a scheme for the library of South Carolina College and a house for H. Denny of Pittsburgh.[67] And he was able to implement it, appropriately, on the facade of the courthouse he designed for Alexandria, Virginia in 1838 (Figures 48-49).[68] Although its function required a different arrangement for the upper floor, the lower plan was much the same as in his South Carolina courthouses, and the dual entrances were similarly articulated with a slight variation. The attached portico was flanked by stairs formed, however, of three short, straight sections linked by curving corner segments. So, he returned to essentially the same facade solution he had forged for his typical South Carolina courthouse in place of developing the purer temple forms of his most sophisticated courthouses. One difference was that the Alexandria Courthouse had a hipped roof surmounted by a central glazed lantern. Although the basic block of the building was square, he could have used a gable roof as he did for his Newburyport, Massachusetts, Custom House, 1833-1835 (Figure 8A). This resembled the redesigned Fairfield and Colleton Courthouses in having a projecting central bay on the entrance facade and the Colleton Courthouse in having a one story portico, lacking a pediment (Figures 6 and 7). The custom house he designed for New Bedford, Massachusetts, at that time had an attached portico with a monumental Doric Order more in his Palladian manner.

Some similarities can be discerned in the chief buildings that Mills later designed or supervised in Washington, D.C., but, given their much larger scale, mainly in terms of plan and structure. The interiors he conceived for the Treasury Building and Patent Office, both begun in 1836, and for his own General Post Office, started three years later, have masonry, cross-vaulted rooms flanking barrel-vaulted halls. The façades of the Treasury and Patent Office may have been inspired by W.P. Elliot (who was paid for the design of each) under the direct influence of A.J. Davis and, latterly, Ithiel Town.[69] Nevertheless, it is noteworthy that the elevation of these buildings on a high basement echoes the Palladianism revived by Mills in his South Carolina courthouses.

The influence of his courthouses and jails has been substantial within South Carolina. And although no contemporary print has been found of them (or, indeed, of those other buildings he designed during the 1820's besides one of the Bethesda Presbyterian Church, Camden; Figure 44), there is evidence of their having affected judicial design in the neighboring states of Georgia and North Carolina, and also the old Southwest, especially Alabama, probably because of the emigration of South Carolinians.[70] Their impact would have been greater had Mills completed the book on his architecture for which he, apparently, assembled a portfolio of drawings, circa 1827-1829, none of which was published in the nineteenth century.[71]

Circumstantial in nature, the evidence for their influence outside his native state is best reviewed first.[72] Their main legacy appears to have been the raised courtroom plan which became more prevalent in the southern and western states from the late 1830's. Among a number of such courthouses with steps to the courtroom inside a full portico were those for Warren and Alexander Counties, North Carolina, 1853 and 1859, and for Wilcox County at Camden, Alabama, 1859. A scattering of more precise imitations of the Mills types have outlasted redevelopment. The second type (an attached portico raised on an arcaded basement and flanked by stairs to the upper courtroom) may have influenced the Camden County Courthouse, Camden,

North Carolina, 1847, and the Pike County Courthouse, Troy, Alabama, dating from the 1860's and, therefore, also attributable to the Italianate taste. The third type (an attached portico raised on a basement spanning the front) was recalled in the Northampton County Courthouse, Jackson, North Carolina, 1859, and the fourth (an attached portico raised on a basement and placed on a longer side) in the Lumpkin County Courthouse, Dahlonega, Georgia, 1838. In 1868 A.B. Mullett, who also served the Federal Government, designed the Post Office and Courthouse at Portland, Maine (completed 1871, but demolished in 1965), with an attached portico raised on an arcaded basement, but without flanking steps, and having more specific Renaissance details.[73]

During Mills's lifetime, his work often formed the basis for designs by other South Carolina architects and master builders; and he can be credited with winning recognition for the profession of architecture as well as for setting high standards of practice.[74] The most direct imitation was the Edgefield Courthouse, 1838-1839 (Figure 54), built by the contractor Charles Beck, who had been earlier associated with Mills commissions.[75] The building has a façade nearly identical with the one designed for Horry Courthouse (Figure 21), other than the substitution of a single flight of steps fronting the portico. Nor is the ground floor fireproof; and its longer sides have four round-headed windows within reveals set into an otherwise unbroken wall, instead of a recessed bay with a triple window. Such imitation of his courthouses has led to misattributions to Mills, notably the present Colleton Courthouse, built 1843-1844 (Figure 52B), to replace the one he had redesigned, after its poorly constructed foundations proved to be unsound.[76] Mills's scheme had neither a raised portico nor outside stairs, whereas the central block of the extant courthouse has an attached tetrastyle portico raised on an arcaded base flanked by curving stairs. His formula has been respected aside from the cruder handling of the details, particularly of the windows, and the absence of fireproofing on the ground floor. An example of rebuilding in the tradition of the South Carolina State House and of Mills's courthouses is the Marion District Courthouse, commissioned in 1851 after the local commissioners of Public Buildings had petitioned for a larger structure. Erected 1853-1854, its entrance facade, if diverging from the Mills pattern in being on a longer side, has a portico with four Tuscan columns raised a full story with curving iron stairs at each end (Figure 55A). Similarly, his Abbeville Courthouse was replaced under an appropriation passed in December 1852 with a templar building fronted by six monumental Greek Doric columns and entablature, apparently combining themes from the facades of his Kershaw Courthouse and its replacement (Figure 25A). But an unprecedented pair of curved stairs extended from a landing at the level of the upper storey and wrapped around the end columns.[77] The later Barnwell Courthouse, constructed between 1878 and 1879, also had a raised portico with curving iron steps attached to a temple-form body (Figure 53B).[78]

A number of other communities throughout the State have comparable Ante-Bellum buildings that demonstrate a widespread use of architectural features popularized by Mills. For example, the Cokesbury Female Seminary, Abbeville District, built in c. 1841 (Figure 56B); the Cheraw Town Hall, Chesterfield District, built 1859 (Figure 55B); and Lance Hall of the Circular Congregational Church, Charleston, opened in 1867 (Figure 58A) all have dual entrances with tetrastyle porticoes, following essentially the same solution Mills had worked out in the 1820's. Then, in 1868, the Legislature granted more authority to county administrations, which tended to increase the complexity of the requirements for courthouses. The growth in population created the need for larger buildings. As prosperity returned to the State late in the nineteenth century most of Mills's courthouses were replaced by more capacious structures in which administrative accommodation took precedence over the courtroom. A few courthouses were fronted with facades derived from the Marlborough prototype, including the 1874 courthouse for Richland County (Figure 58B). One Mills building, the Williamsburg Courthouse, has been made to resemble the Horry Courthouse by the addition of stairs to its front; and another architect's building, the formerly Victorian courthouse for Aiken, has been made to resemble Mills's Marlborough type by the addition of an attached portico and exterior stairs (Figure 57).[79] Otherwise, in the late nineteenth and early twentieth centuries, the gable-ended form with a separate, attached portico once again became increasingly confined to church architecture.

Perhaps no nineteenth century architect was more influenced by Mills than his fellow Charlestonian, Edward Brickell White (1806-1882). White's Chester Courthouse, begun 1852 (Figure 24B), closely resembles Mills's courthouses for Georgetown and Williamsburg in having a full temple form fronted by an hexastyle portico on an arcaded basement (Figures 22 and 23 and compare 24A).[80] White added porticoes to two already constructed buildings in order to achieve greater monumentality and he borrowed Mills's stair and entrance compositions for more convenient access. One of these was the main section of the College of Charleston (originally designed by William Strickland), on the south front of which in 1850 he placed a portico with a monumental order elevated on a full story arcaded basement, framed by curving stairs (Figure 43A).[81] That year he also attached a portico raised a full story onto his own Charleston High School. Here he concealed the stairs, as Mills had done for the Williamsburg Courthouse. Millsian, too, is the emphasis that White gave to both the upper and lower entrances of the Charleston Market Hall, 1841 (Figure 53A), with a more Italianate arrangement of two flights of steps over the lower archway.

One twentieth century architect was profoundly influenced by Mills. Albert Simons, F.A.I.A. (1890-1980), restored several Mills buildings during nearly seven decades of architectural practice and gained a first-hand appreciation of Mills's ability. In one of his firm's finest designs, dating from 1932 to 1938, he raised the gymnasium of the College of Charleston a full story to provide locker rooms and storage below (equivalent to the offices in Mills's courthouses) and fronted it with four engaged, Greek Doric columns standing on an arcaded basement. His Memminger Auditorium, designed in 1938, has much the same massing and a portico with two Greek Doric columns *in antis*, akin to Mills's Monumental Church, flanked by stairs. (Although the columns are raised a full story, the Auditorium floor slopes down to almost ground level at the rear). Numerous other buildings by the firm of Simons and Lapham have details freely adapted from Mills's courthouses, as well as other of his buildings.

* * * * * * * * *

The years that Mills spent in South Carolina in the third decade of the century enabled him to experiment and to develop interests beyond architecture, but without improving his financial standing. His South Carolina architecture was so little known elsewhere in the period that his national reputation was not enhanced. He had gained experience in public service and its manifold impediments to architectural excellence, anticipating the melancholy course of his work for the Federal Government. Yet he considered that he had fulfilled a personal obligation, writing in a letter, dated 30 September 1827, "I shall have the satisfaction to think that I have in some measure paid the debt of gratitude to the state that gave me birth by the execution of the works I have done."[82]

NOTES

[1] This study is based largely on manuscript sources in the South Carolina Department of Archives and History, Columbia (hereafter cited as SCDAH). Most useful of these sources were journals, ledgers, and vouchers of the Treasury Department, Upper and Lower Divisions (the journals and ledgers are available on microfilm and are cited as SCDAH mfm); petitions to the Legislature by local Commissioners of Public Buildings (hereafter, CPB), contractors, and others; grand jury presentments; Legislative committee reports; specifications; bonds; drawings; and correspondence of the Board of Public Works (hereafter BPW) and of the Superintendent of Public Works (hereafter SPW). All of Mills's courthouse and jail plans are missing from the SCDAH and seem to have been systematically removed. Mills may have retained some of them as his personal propety as many public officials did with their records. Except for the Asylum drawings, which had been lent to another state in the 19th century, almost all specifications, agreements, and similar documents relating to Mills's South Carolina public buildings are also missing from an unusually complete set of state records. Even documents required to be attached to bonds have been removed. Someone evidently went through and attempted to collect everything attributable to Mills's hand; numerous drawings and specifications by other architects are present. Mills himself may have done so to provide material for his planned "Architectural Works of Robert Mills" (H.M. Pierce Gallagher, *Robert Mills, Architect of the Washington Monument, 1781-1855* [New York, 1935], 168-171; heieafter Gallagher, *Mills*). He was requested to "furnish" receipts, a contract, and specifications to settle a claim in 1826 (SCDAH 10-3-1826-77), indicating that some public documents were in his possession after his official capacities had ceased. Many of Mills's papers are said to have been lost through a fire in Texas (Gallagher, *Mills*, 23). All major groups known to his Evans and Dimitry descendants are preserved in public archives.

The SCDAH manuscript sources are supplemented by *Acts and Resolutions of the General Assembly of the State of South Carolina* (Columbia; hereafter cited as *Acts* with the date of the session rather than the date of publication); by *The Statutes at Large of South Carolina* . . . (1836 - present, cited as *Stat.* with the volume number preceeding and the page number following [e.g., 5 *Stat.* 376]); by the separately printed annual reports of the BPW and SPW collected by David Kohn and Bess Glenn in *Internal Improvement in South Carolina, 1817-1828* (Washington, 1938; hereafter *Improvement*) and by Robert Mills's own *Statistics of South Carolina, Including a View of its Natural, Civil and Military History, General and Particular* (Columbia, 1826; hereafter, Mills, *Statistics*). Other sources for individual buildings are included in the appendix and often are not cited in the text. In the notes and appendix, courthouse is abbreviated CH and jail is abbreviated J.

Previous studies of Mills's courthouses and jails have made only tentative attributions. Fiske Kimball ("Robert Mills," *Dictionary of American Biography* [New York, 1934] XII, 11) lists four of Mills's sixteen South Carolina courthouses and three of his twelve jails excluding one for York, for which no evidence has been found to attribute it to Mills (see Appendix I); Gallagher (*Mills*, 43) lists three courthouses and no jails, (no source cited).

Beatrice St. Julien Ravenel (*Architects of Charleston* [Charleston, 1964 rev.], 125; hereafter, Ravenel, *Architects*) gives the same list as Kimball and notes that it is from an advertisement in the *Charleston Courier*, 21 February 1822. She adds five other courthouses for a total of nine (excluding the existing Colleton courthouse, incorrectly attributed on the basis of its design. The existing wing of the Charleston jail is also incorrectly attributed to Mills). Blanche Marsh (*Robert Mills, Architect in South Carolina* [Columbia, 1970]) lists eight courthouses (excluding four incorrectly attributed; she illustrates later buildings for Colleton and Spartanburg and includes Lancaster and Edgefield, which are by others) and two jails (excluding York and Charleston).

For courthouse architecture generally, see Nikolaus Pevsner, *A History of Building Types* (Princeton, N.J., 1976), 52-62 (including town halls; hereafter, Pevsner, *Building Types*), and in the United States, Richard Pare, ed., *Courthouse: A Photographic Document* (New York, 1978). An important regional study is Marcus Whiffen, "The Early County Courthouses of Virginia," *Journal of the Society of Architectural Historians* (hereafter *JSAH*), vol. 18 (1959), no. 5, 2-10.

[2] Statistical analyses of Mills's buildings, of earlier buildings which he replaced, and of later buildings which replaced his own are given in footnote 74 herein. Information on individual buildings is given in the Appendix by district in alphabetical order, and the dates of construction are summarized in Figure 60. For locations, see the State map by Mills (Figure 59).

In autobiographical notes, Mills states that "South Carolina having given him an invitation to aid in perfecting her internal improvements, he accepted and in 1820 removed with his family to that state, receiving the appointment of engineer and architect of the state and a commissioned seat in the board of commissions of public works." (Gallagher, *Mills*, 161). Since the Legislature elected him late in December of 1820, he probably accomplished little in the State before 1821 (SCDAH MS "Journal of the Senate . . ." p. 224-225). On 16 June 1820 he had written to ask Thomas Jefferson to recommend him to the governor of Virginia as state engineer, and he said that he had little employment in Baltimore because of "the great depression of commerce" (*Presidential Papers Microfilm, Thomas Jefferson Papers* [Washington, 1974], reel 52; hereafter Jefferson, *Presidential Papers*). Mills remained in South Carolina for most of the next nine years until 1829, when he left to return briefly to Baltimore to raise the Causici statue atop the Washington Monument (Maryland Historical Society, MS 871, Box 1). He remained in the North and took a house in Washington on 1 May 1830 (diary entries quoted in Hennig Cohen [ed.], "The Journal of Robert Mills, 1828-1830," *South Carolina Historical and Genealogical Magazine*, vol. 53 [1952], 100; [hereafter Cohen, "Journal"]).

Mills received his professional training primarily under Benjamin Henry Latrobe between c. 1804 and 1812 (Edward C. Carter II, and Thomas E. Jeffrey, *The Papers of Benjamin Henry Latrobe*; The Micro Text Edition [Clifton, N.J., 1976], 35/G5, 98/D3, and 101/B14; hereafter, *Latrobe* mfm). Mills was doing drafting work for Latrobe earlier, but not in his office (Henning Cohen, "An Unpublished Diary by Robert Mills, 1803," *South Carolina Historical and Genealogical Magazine*, vol. 51 [1950], 190-193. Mills credited Latrobe with reversing all his ideas on architecture [Jefferson, *Presidential Papers*, letter of 3 Oct. 1806]). Mills's correspondence with Jefferson does not support the assertion that Jefferson tutored him, and Mills does not state this in his autobiographical writings (Gallagher, *Mills*, 158, 159, 168-169). On 13 June 1808, he asked Jefferson for a recommendation because he intended to begin his own practice, but he continued his association with Latrobe for at least four more years. For "about two years," beginning in 1800, Mills had worked in the office of James Hoban, "architect of the public buildings" in Washington (William Dunlap, *A History of the Rise and Progress of the Arts of Design in the United States* [New York, 1969 reprint], II, 221 [hereafter, Dunlap, *History*]; see Gallagher, *Mills*, 158). He afterwards travelled extensively in the United States and on his return was befriended by Jefferson, who lent him some of his architectural books and who "engaged" him to prepare drawings of Monticello (*ibid.*, 169); Mills states that Jefferson's library contained "some few works of eminent Roman architects, but no Grecian writers," indicating that he probably did not have access to all of his books (*Antiquities of Athens*, vol. I, for example, was in the library along with more than a few other architectural books; William Bainter O'Neal, *Jefferson's Fine Arts Library; His Selection for the University of Virginia Together With His Own Architectural Books* [Charlottesville, 1976]).

Before 1820 for Charleston, Mills designed the Circular Congregational Church (1804-1806) and the First Baptist Church (drawing dated 1818; constructed 1819-1822). For Augusta, Georgia, he designed the First Presbyterian Church in 1807. For Burlington, N.J., he designed a prison in 1808. For Philadelphia, where he lived from 1806-1815, he designed Washington Hall (1809-1816), Franklin Row (drawing dated 1809), the Sansom Street Baptist Church (1811-1812), the Schuylkill Bridge (1813-1814; in collaboration with its engineer Lewis Wernwag), and the Octagon Unitarian Church (1812-1813). For Richmond, he designed the Monumental Church (cornerstone laid 4 Aug. 1812). For Baltimore, where he resided from 1815-1820, he designed the monumental column to George Washington (designed 1814), Waterloo Row (1816-1819), the First Baptist Church (designed 1816), and St. John's Evangelical Episcopal Church (1817-1818). For information about these commissions, see the manuscript minutes of the Circular Church, Charleston; David Moltke-Hansen (ed.), *Art in the Lives of South Carolinians; Nineteenth Century Chapters* (Charleston, 1978-1979; hereafter Moltke-Hansen, *Art*); John Morrill Bryan, *An Unpublished Diary and Early Drawings, the Results of Recent Research: Robert Mills, Architect, 1781-1855* (Columbia, 1976; hereafter Bryan, *Mills*); Gallagher, *Mills*; Ravenel, *Architects*, 116-135; Lee H. Nelson, *Robert Mills — Architect and Engineer, 1781-1855; A Brief Chronology of His Activities While in Philadelphia* (n.p., 1962); Kenneth Ames, "Robert Mills and The Philadelphia Row House," *JSAH*, vol. 27 (1968), 140-146; William Voss Elder, III, *Robert Mills' Waterloo Row — Baltimore 1816* (Baltimore, 1971); and Richard Xavier Evans (ed.), "The Daily Journal of Robert Mills, Baltimore, 1816" *Maryland Historical Magazine*, XXX (1935), 257-271; records of the Lancaster-Schuylkill Bridge, Pennsylvania Historical Society; Washington Monument Papers, Maryland Historical Society; J. Jefferson Miller II, "The Designs for the Washington Monument in Baltimore," *JSAH*, Vol. 23 (1964), 19-28; and Richard X. Evans, "The Washington Monument in Baltimore; Robert Mills, Architect," *The Federal Architect*, Oct. 1973, 38-41. (The Richmond City Hall and Courthouse, a major commission, is omitted because it was redesigned by Godefroy; for Mills's design, see Robert L. Alexander, "Maximilian Godefroy in Virginia; A French Interlude in Richmond's Architecture," *The Virginia Magazine of History and Biography*, vol. 69 [1961], 420-431; fig. 3). For Mills's residence in Philadelphia, Nelson cites city directories. The files of the Museum of Early Southern Decorative Arts, Winston-Salem, N.C., cite city directories for Baltimore and contemporary information from newspapers on several commissions (Dunlap, *History*, II, 223, gives 1817 as the date he moved).

[3] Letter to Robert Gilmor (President of the Board of Managers of the Washington Monument). Maryland Historical Society, Washington Monument Papers, MS 876, Box I; in a postscript he lamented, "I wish it were in my power to rest where I am, but you know my dear sir what the state of things is in Baltimore in my line of business — I have got tired of an intenerant life; and when I set down in Baltimore I *anticipated* a settlement. The unfortunate turn of things here has ruined my prospects, and left me nothing of all my earnings for the years past." Earlier, on 20 April, when seeking an advance on his annual fees for supervising the construction of the monument, he had pleaded, "I have no business bringing me in anything, and should you deny me this favor, I shall know not how to obtain means to go to market." All quotations are given verbatim except that sentences are occasionally separated.

[4] In December 1818 the Legislature appropriated one million dollars to be spent on improvements in transportation over a four year period; the construction of a large number of public buildings coincided with this program but was an essentially separate endeavor, even though the same agencies bore responsibility for all construction between 1818 and

1822. The nation-wide enthusiasm for internal improvements was a state-by-state effort to concentrate as much trade as possible. For a contemporary overview, see H.S. Tanner, *Memoir on the Recent Surveys, Observations, and Internal Improvements, in the United States* (Philadelphia, 1829).

[5] The most important act to provide for pre-1820 courthouses and jails was passed on 21 December 1799 and authorized courthouses and gaols for twenty districts, each to cost $5,000 (5 *Stat.* 376, 7 *Stat.* 291f). This act also provided for repairs to the existing courthouses and jails of Georgetown, Orangeburg, Beaufort and Camden (created as four of the original seven districts in 1769; SCDAH MS Acts, 29 July 1769; see David Duncan Wallace, *The History of South Carolina* [New York, 1934], 47-65). The Charleston Courthouse was in repair, thus accounting for the total of twenty-five districts which existed as of 1 January 1800 (7 *Stat.* 291f; the twenty which were intended in the appropriation may be determined by deducting the five listed here). Many of these districts were based on boundaries created for thirty-four counties in 1785 (4 *Stat.* 661f; cf. 561f and 564f). Three additional districts were created between 1801 and 1805. (5 *Stat.* 497; Horry, Lexington, and Williamsburg) making the twenty eight districts that are included in Mills's 1825 Atlas (see Mills's map of South Carolina, Figure 59 herein, and *Mills's Atlas; Atlas of the State of South Carolina, 1825* (Easley, S.C., 1980). One other district was added to the total in 1826, when Anderson and Pickens were created by dividing Pendleton.

Mills provides detailed information on each district in his *Statistics*. In a table on page 211, he gives the areas and population served by each of the twenty-eight district seats which existed in 1820. The areas range from 486 to 2,112 square miles and average 1,079; the populations range from 5,025 to 80,212 and average 17,948.

[6] *Improvement*, 25, 39. For the creation of the office of Civil and Military Engineer and of the Board of Public Works, see 6 *Stat.* 58-60, 124-128, 189, 202-203; *Acts*, 1824, 120. Because the Legislature met at the end of each year, the actual date of creation for these offices was in December of the years before the initial years given here.

[7] Wilson's main responsibility was to supervise the construction of canals and roads. Wilson (1789-1832) was educated as an engineer at the University of Edinburgh and achieved renown more for his defenses of Charleston during the War of 1812, his map of the State in 1822, and his subsequent work as a railway engineer in Pennsylvania than for his two years of service as Civil and Military Engineer. He wished to be an acting commissioner, but despite his unrivaled qualifications and dedicated service, the Legislature used him as a scapegoat for public dissatisfaction with an ill-conceived program (biographical sketch in "The Railroad Men of America," *Magazine of Western History*, c. 1888, p. 67-75; letter by Wilson to J.R. Poinsett, 31 January 1820 in SCHS Arnoldus Vanderhorst Papers.)

[8] Blanding (1776-1839) was successively a school teacher, lawyer, public administrator, bank president, and railroad developer. He was not an architect and as SPW he did not supervise the construction of courthouses and jails (see *Improvement*, 599, for a biographical sketch of this prominent Columbia citizen and 227-586 for his reports).

[9] Cohen, "Journal," 219 (1951).

[10] For information on Jay's life and work, see Thomas Gamble, "Romance of Wm. Jay, Savannah Architect; His Genius Is Reflected in Buildings Here." *Savannah Morning News*, 8 May 1932, and "Tracking Down a Will-O'-the-Wisp; Just How It Is Done, Thomas Gamble's Pursuit of Elusive William Jay," *Ibid.*, 11 May 1932; James Vernon McDonough, "William Jay, Regency Architect in Georgia and South Carolina" (Princeton U. dissertation, 1950; hereafter McDonough, "Jay"); and Ravenel, *Architects*, 107-115.

The report of the Civil & Military Engineer for 1818 refers to plans marked a, b, and c for a Beaufort courthouse (not used) and others marked d, e, and f for a wooden courthouse for Barnwell (actually built). His 1819 report recommends using plans d, e, f for Chester and plans a, b, c, or d, e, f, for Fairfield, (*Improvement*, A2-A3, 2-3, 25 and 38). At least two sets of standard courthouse plans were thus being used at the time.

[11] SCDAH, BPW Letterbook, 2, 4-5. For examples of earlier plans, see Figure 31.

[12] *Southern Patriot and Commercial Advertiser*, 4 February 1820. Cited in Ravenel,

Architects, 110.

[13] Although the Sumter Courthouse was executed to Jay's designs, it was later rebuilt (Figures 10-11), and its courtroom was moved to the second story (in 1839-1840; SCDAH Bond dated 1 July 1839). Mills called the Sumter Courthouse and jail "handsome," an adjective he usually reserved for his own work (*Statistics*, 742).

The initial payment for the Chester Courthouse was in April 1820 (SCDAH mfm 7-7B135), and in December 1820 work was expected to be completed early in 1821 (*Improvement*, 27). An undated petition by the contractor, William Turner, states only that some alteration had been "made by authority of Captn. Baker" (SCDAH, 10-3-ND-521).

Funds for a Beaufort courthouse had been approved by 1819 (*Improvement*, 1-2). This courthouse was a two-storey, 40' x 50' building with a glazed, pan-tile roof (*ibid.*, 26-27; SCDAH, Plans of Buildings, MB17-17).

The Beaufort design resembles Jay's Bullock House and Savannah Theatre more than his best known dwelling designs (Figure 1). The lesser known buildings had hipped roofs with pediments. The Beaufort fenestration is typical of his work (see McDonough, "Jay" p. 31-32). Although the Beaufort drawing is probably earlier than the set he prepared and although it does not conform exactly to his Colleton and Sumter specifications, the basic features are essentially the same. The Savannah Theatre opened 4 December 1818 and was described on 9 December as having a "semi-circular" interior and large lobbies, features which the Beaufort Courthouse appears to have emulated (although McDonough interprets the description in a way that makes this less likely; his 59-61 and figs. 91 and 100). The modified amphitheatral plan of Jay's courthouses made their width broader than their depth.

Mills had earlier used fenestration similar to Jay's for his prison at Burlington, New Jersey (Gallagher, *Mills*, opp. 24). Charleston's City Hall, built in c. 1800 as a branch of the Bank of the U.S., also has similar fenestration except that its second floor windows are within reveals. Although reveals were commonly used by Latrobe and others, Jay's use was distinctive, and Mills's Fireproof Building appears to reproduce Jay's usage.

Funds for the Pendleton jail were appropriated in December 1818 (*Acts*, 98) and the initial payment was made in June 1819 (SCDAH mfm 7-7B132). Its specifications call for a two story building 45' x 35', with a tile roof. The Colleton jail was to be of identical size.

[14] SCDAH, Public Improvement, 1800-1830, Buildings, Receipts, 1820. The receipt notes that each set of courthouse designs included eight drawings and that the sets were "furnished Mr. Baker — and Major Wilson." In addition to plans and elevations, at least one full-size cornice profile was included for the courtroom (mentioned in the Colleton and Sumter specifications). Jay was paid $75 for the courthouse design, $75 for the jail design, and $25 for each set of drawings (a total of $300). These were evidently new designs and were different from those referred to in the SPB's reports (*Improvement*, 2-3. Cf. note 10), and the drawings reproduced as Figures 4-5 were probably part of one set (SCL A/8317).

The Colleton specifications are signed by the contractor William N. Thompson, and by Wilson and Baker, who are specified on Jay's receipt to have received his designs (preceeding paragraph). Specifications for both a new courthouse and a new jail are included, and the courthouse specifications are nearly identical in content, format, and handwriting to the Sumter courthouse specifications.

[15] While providing designs for buildings for the BPW, Mills was also involved in work on roads and canals (SCDAH Reports ND-104-05 and SPW [sic] letterbook, 1820-1827, 95-100, 171; *Improvement*, 170-175, for an 1822 report signed by him; SCHS Mills papers, 6-7 March 1821 letters to his wife.) However, Abram Blanding had charge of supervising the construction of roads and canals before Mills came onto the Board and after the Board was abolished, and he also submitted reports during the two years that Mills was on the Board. In an autobiographical sketch, Mills credits himself only with having "designed and erected a series of locks between the canal and the river at the foot of the hill on which the City of Columbia was built " (Gallagher, *Mills*, 161). Mills wrote two pamphlets on canals (*A Treatise on Inland Navigation* . . . [Baltimore, 1820] and *Inland Navigation, Plan for a Great*

Canal Between Charleston and Columbia . . . [Columbia, 1821]). He was interested and qualified, but he had a small part in this work in South Carolina. The major projects had been begun in 1818, about three years before he joined the Board, and were still incomplete when he joined, so no further major projects could be undertaken. After 1822, he was not involved with this work. He has been blamed repeatedly and unfairly for the failure of projects which he did not initiate and over which he exercised little or no supervision.

The lockkeeper's lodge for Landsford Canal has been attributed to Mills, but its contract predates his election to the Board of Public Works (1 November 1820; SCDAH 10-3-ND-980). Robert Leckie agreed to construct a stone building with minimum dimensions specified, and as a highly expert stonemason, he is likely to have provided the design. (Subsequently, Leckie was contractor for the York Courthouse. For further biographical information, see E. Thomas 'Crowson, "Building the Landsford Canal," *South Carolina History Illustrated*, Vol. 1 [1970], 18-22, 59-61).

[16] *Improvement*, 108-115 and 120. The entire report is signed by "Robert Mills" and by three other Board members, including "Robert G. Mills," who was from Chester District (*ibid.*, p. 128; 1820 Census). No new construction was begun in 1821 because of an oversight in the legislation (*Improvement*, 110).

[17] This drawing is on the reverse of Jay's specifications for the Colleton Courthouse (Appendix II, 1). Jay's Colleton and Sumter specifications call for first stories 18' high and second stories 12' high; the Beaufort elevation reflects these relative proportions. The CPB report for 1821 states that "with the consent of the contractor and his securities (for his bond), a change has been made in the plan of the courthouse, by which all of the offices are placed in the basement story" (*Improvement*, 111; cf. 109). For complaints about ground-floor courtrooms, see the Appendix herein for Barnwell and Colleton; cf. Sumter.

[18] Thompson praises and approves Mills's revised plan in a letter dated 29 June 1821. He also refers to a portico being added (SCDAH, Internal Improvement Files, Buildings; cited in Evelyn McD. Frasier, "The Colleton County Courthouse," *South Carolina History Illustrated*, Vol. 1 [1970], 23-25, 66-68, and in Ann Fripp Hampton, "History of the Colleton County Courthouse," *Historic Courthouses of South Carolina: Colleton County*, [Columbia, 1980], 8). Although Jay used one-bay, one-story porticos on his Savannah houses (Figure 1 herein), he did not specify them for his Colleton or Sumter Courthouses. A portico of this type appears on the Colleton sketch, but not on the Fairfield sketch which was to have conformed with Colleton (*Improvement*, 111), but funds were inadequate. Although Jay made this type of portico something of a trademark, it was a standard feature of the time, and Mills had used it earlier, for example, on the sides of his Monumental Church, Richmond (which also have large fanlights the width of the portico and directly above, another feature that Jay used and may have acquired independently).

One other feature which Jay often used is a one-bay central pavilion, which occurs in the drawing of Colleton and Fairfield and which is still to be seen behind the added, monumental portico of the Fairfield Courthouse (Figure 8B). Three-bay, central pavilions were common in Georgian dwellings; one-bay examples are rare for any period, but do occur, for example, on the Wickham house, Richmond, a building often attributed to Mills; whether or not it is by him, it is an earlier example that he knew (it has a one-bay, one-story portico as well and a boldly simplified tri-part front). The origin of this unusual feature may be from the facade of a church with a pavilion the maximum width of its steeple, specifically the steeple of Mills's First Presbyterian Church, Augusta, designed by him in 1807 (Bryan, *Diary*, 15-16). A comparison of Jay's earliest American house with a later example suggests that he was more indebted to Mills than Mills to Jay (Figure 1), even to the use of details such as the partially fluted, archaic Greek Doric columns (which Mills adopted from Latrobe, who used them as early as 1792 for Hammerwood Lodge, Sussex, England, and who later used them to support the rotunda floor of the Capitol and for his proposed Tayloe house, which was to have a one-story portico; cf. Talbot Hamlin, *Benjamin Henry Latrobe* [New York, 1955], pls. 2 & 7 [hereafter, Hamlin *Latrobe*]). Mills used this column for his Monumental Church and other buildings. Even Jay's placement of his main cornice between the first and second floors in place of a string course may have been derived from Mills (cf. Gallagher, *Mills*, opp. 88 (right) and opp. 82 (portico), although he could also have adapted Palladio's usage independently. Mills does seem to have borrowed some features from Jay, but not the apsidal entrance to the secondary front of Ainsley Hall's house (whose main floor plan he borrowed from Latrobe; cf. Hamlin, *Latrobe*, figs. 25 & 11, and James C. Massey, "Robert Mills Documents, 1823: A House for Ainsley Hall in Columbia, South Carolina," *JSAH*, Vol. 22 [1963], fig. 4). In any case, Mills's houses are more in the tradition of American domestic architecture, and Jay's are more in the tradition of British public architecture. The assumption that the Colleton design is essentially the creation of Mills makes his later use of the design more explicable. His custom house for Newburyport, Massachusetts (Gallagher, *Mills*, opp. 58) has a one-story, one-bay portico centered on a one-bay, two-story central projection for a three-by-three bay, temple-form building.

[19] This drawing (Fig. 8A) is one among the papers of Robert Mills in the special collections division of the Howard-Tilton Memorial Library, Tulane University, and it is captioned "Views of the New and Old Courthouse, Winnsboro" (the district seat for Fairfield; the caption is given in Gallagher, *Mills*, 167. The drawing forms part of a series, some of which are dated 1821-1823).

A petition by the contractor, William McCreight & Sons, states that "a material alteration in the plan of the House was proposed to your petitioners by Mr. Mills . . . ," requiring additional materials (see footnote 18). These include bricks for "Gable ends," a further indication that the original plan called for a hip roof. Mills also added brick partitions and extra steps (SCDAH 10-3-n.d.-531).

[20] Adequate provisions for the maintenance of courthouses were never fully implemented during the Ante-Bellum Period. Since courthouses were constructed with state funds and since the Legislature provided for major repairs, they were considered state buildings by local inhabitants, and they were intentionally neglected until defects magnified to the point of requiring major repairs. (See *Improvement*, 109, 113, 161-162, and Herbert A. Johnson, "Courthouse Design Financing, and Maintenance in Ante-Bellum South Carolina," in Moltke-Hansen, *Art*).

[21] Jay's Beaufort Courthouse had stairs inside at the front of the building, and his courtroom could be kept closed when it was not in use, but offices of some earlier courthouses such as Darlington (Fig. 31) and Barnwell could not be reached without passing through the courtroom (see Appendix I).

[22] *Improvement*, 31 and 110. The original appropriation was in December 1819. Since another appropriation could not be made until December 1820, when the Legislature met again and when Mills was appointed to the BPW, Jay's plans were not used. An undated letter by Mills requests that he be sent the Marlborough courthouse and jail plans because the Boards wanted them revised "to endeavor to bring the cost of buildings within the appropriation" (SCDAH Letterbook, SPW, 1822-1827, 170).

[23] Page 631-632. By "characteristic," Mills was presumably referring to the fenestration, the most distinctive feature of the Union J and of the other jails which will be shown to have been similar.

[24] *Improvement*, 109 and 36. Since jails were usually for short-term confinement, he did not provide rooms for solitary confinement or for work. His addition to the Charleston "jail" was a prison wing, which had a cell designed as a sleeping area for each individual.

In 1806 Mills had submitted plans for a State penitentiary to Governor Hamilton (7 July; SCDAH Reports, 1807-50-61; cf. SCDAH 1808-79 and 1807-50-01/143 for related documentation, including a letter from Latrobe advocating mild corrective measures). See also his plans for the Burlington County, N.J. "Debtor's Gaol and Work-House for Felons," May 1808 (Gallagher, *Mills*, opp. 24 and 26; also 200-203, 209-210. On 203, Mills refers to "the justly celebrated Howard," the English prison reformer John Howard (1726-1790), who advocated solitary confinement and rehabilitative work [*Encyclopeida Britannica*, 11th ed. For prison architecture generally, see Pevsner, *Building Types*, 159-168.]). In a forthcoming article for the *South Carolina Historical Magazine*, John Bryan discusses Mills's indebtedness to Jefferson and Latrobe for ideas on penitentiaries. Mills also designed a penitentiary for New Orleans (*Statistics*, 467n). For an example of the severity of confinement in 1820, see Appendix I under Edgefield.

[25] The Greenville courthouse (Fig. 16) is illustrated in an 1825 view of the village by Joshua Tucker (Abby Aldrich Rockefeller Folk Art Collection, Williamsburg; Francis W. Bilodeau, Mrs. Thomas J. Tobias, and E. Milby Burton, *Art in South Carolina 1670-1970* ([Charleston, 1970]; reproduced there as Fig. 117 (cited hereafter, Bilodeau, *Art*).

The Newberry Courthouse is described in detail by J.C. Carwile, *Reminiscences of Newberry* (Charleston, 1890), 72-73.

[26] *Statistics*, 772.

[27] Alsobrook, the contractor, requested permission to double the height of the roof from one-sixth to one-third of its width (SCDAH, Internal Improvement Files, 303-4; request dated 25 June 1822. The existing building and payment records indicate that permission was granted; SCDAH, 10-4-1824-149, & mfm 7-7C-93). The original roof would not have accommodated usable rooms in the attic; the increased height allowed for additional cells. Otherwise, the design can be attributed to Mills on the basis of its originality and its handling of details such as the fenestration. Alsobrook's courthouse for Lancaster is a provincial version of a Mills courthouse.

The form of the gable is unusual for South Carolina and is probably by Mills. It differs from the more common, stepped gable in having sloping sides; and it differs from the usual raked-blocking course in reversing the position of the sloping elements. This distinctive form shows, for example, on the ends of the Pennsylvania Statehouse (Independence Hall), for which Mills had provided additions (Gallagher, *Mills*, opp. 46), and is relatively common in the North.

[28] The surviving specifications for the Edgefield jail state that it was to be "... in every particular & after the model of the Union jail ... " (Appendix II, 5). Each story was ten feet in height. The illustration of the destroyed Spartanburg jail is from the WPA *History of Spartanburg County* (n.p., 1940), opp. 209. It resembled Union's form except in having end pavilions, but the detailing differed considerably (having a rough surface, quoins, a string course, end windows below, and larger end windows above). Several other jails will be mentioned that were built using essentially the same plans and specification, but without vaulting.

[29] Written from Columbia, this letter indicates that Mills was responsible for paying the contractors for at least some of the canal construction; South Carolina Historical Society, Mills Papers, 11-517.

[30] The creation of a separate SPB was proposed by the Committee on Internal Improvement on 21 December 1822 as part of a lengthy report summarizing the reasons so little had been accomplished in four years with $1 million. (*Acts*, 1822, 95-100; cf. 49).

[31] SCDAH, Reports, 1822-109-11f. This report appears to be in Mills's handwriting, and its content and his position at the time make an attribution to him almost certain.

An attempt was made at the end of 1822 to tighten the bidding process. To prevent contractors from knowing how much had been appropriated for a building and from bidding the full amount, the Legislature published only the total appropriation for all buildings (SCDAH, Reports, 1822-109-11).

[32] Furthermore, Mills was then supervising the repair of buildings in Columbia (S.C. College); Darlington (courthouse and jail); Georgetown, Horry, Kershaw, and Lexington (courthouses); and Marion, Richland and Charleston (jails); *Acts*, 1822, 102.

[33] McIver is not known to have practiced as an architect. He worked as a contractor on the Sumter jail, and he later worked as an engineer building railroads. His qualifications were good, but so much inferior to Mills's that political influence is likely to have caused the change (as is suggested in the *Charleston Courier*, 8 May 1823). McIver was the brother of a prominent State Senator.

[34] *Acts,* 1824, 14.

[35] For example, the Fairfield Courthouse required appropriations of $12,000 (*Improvement*, 2, 111) and was not fireproof. The standard appropriation for Mills's courthouses with fireproof ground floors was $10,000 (SCDAH, Reports 1821-99 and 1822-110; cf. footnote 46). The defense of Mills is quoted in Ravenel, *Architects*, 123-124. Another article in the *Courier* of 8 May 1823 states that Mills "was unaccountably removed from his place by a vote of the Legislature, at a very late hour of a very oppressive session . . . ."

[36] Maryland Historical Society, Washington Monument Papers, MS 876, Box I.

[37] *Mills' Atlas of the State of South Carolina, 1825* (reprinted, Easley, S.C., 1980), with an introduction by Gene Waddell ("Robert Mills, Cartographer").

[38] *Statistics*, 591, although his elevation (frontispiece herein) shows an attached portico with four Ionic columns. In the descriptions quoted, he refers to a full portico of six Ionic columns. That six were actually built is said to be confirmed by the survival of the capitals in Camden (Thomas J. Kirkland and Robert M. Kennedy, *Historic Camden, Part Two, Nineteenth Century* [Columbia, 1926], 257). The extensively renovated building survives and is recorded in HABS drawings (S.C. 13-9; partially reproduced herein as Figs. 26-28).

[39] That the entire third story was floored is implied by the reduction called for in the thickness of the wall, by the number and size of tables for juries (four each 3' x 10', the overall size of the building was 50' x 40' (the size of Jay's courthouses, which had the same orientation), and by the number and size of the windows. The orientation is implied by the position of the hall and the overall dimensions (see Appendix II, 6A).

[40] SCDAH Bonds, dated 7 March 1825. An accompanying bill for extra work by the contractor states "deduct for difference of iron not put into the building as contracted for . . . ." Thus, part of Mills's reinforcement was deemed unnecessary (dated 29 October 1827). In an undated petition for payment (10-3-ND-433), the contractor, John C. Chapman, Jr., has the effrontery to state that "had your petitioner erected the building according to the plan of his contract it would have been of little value to the state and would have been in danger of falling down." On 2 November 1827 he was paid the full $1,400 he requested (all but $3.34 of the $10,000 appropriation). The extra payment was primarily to add two feet to the height of the first and third stories and to increase the pitch of the roof, significantly altering the proportions of Mills's design. In 1831 Chapman requested yet another appropriation of $1,005.84, and on 3 December the Legislature's Joint Committee on Public Buildings recommended rejection; this time, he was not paid.

[41] About 1825, Mills probably designed "an extensive citadel, or fortified arsenal and barracks," which in 1826 was being erected on the present Marion Square in Charleston (*Statistics*, 421n; see also SCDAH 10-4-1822-68 and 10-3-1825-24). Mills notes further that "the works will be guarded by bastions at the four angles, on which cannon will be mounted . . . ." The building was being completed in 1830 (Ravenel, *Architects*, 142). It still stands, but its original two stories have been increased to four. The design of this structure has been ascribed to Frederick Wesner, but it does not resemble his other known work (*ibid.*, 136-146; he was the contractor, however. [SCDAH Vouchers, 21 July 1827]). On the other hand, it does resemble work by Mills and the work of C.N. Ledoux, whose work may have influenced Mills via Latrobe, but whose designs are not reflected in Wesner's small body of work. The Old Citadel (formerly the South Carolina Military College) has a central court on three sides of which were built arcades similar to the one Ledoux designed for the Barrière de Fontainbleau, Paris (with the arches resting on abacuses without an entablature and with unfluted columns whose breadth was about one fifth of their height, features more Romanesque than Classical (cf. Rich Bornemann, "Some Ledoux-inspired Buildings in America," *JSAH*, Vol. 13 [1957], 15-17). The arches and columns of the Citadel court strongly resemble the arches and columns at the foot of Mills's stairs on the ground floor of the south wing of the Patent Office. The corner "bastions" have equivalents in the end pavilions of Latrobe's Philadelphia Bank (Gothic), for which Mills supervised the construction during 1807-1808 (Gallagher, *Mills*, opp. 46, top). Latrobe gave Mills "Brittons Gothic Antiquities" on 13 February 1808 (*Latrobe* mfm, 62F1). Gallagher notes this as John Britton's *Architectural Antiquities of Great Britain* (London, from 1807), a work which contains Romanesque

as well as Gothic architecture. The corner towers of Mills's marine hospital designs are comparable, one of which has columns with similar proportions (Gallagher, *Mills*, opp. 60). As early as 1824, Mills expressed an appreciation for the "heavy simplicity of the Saxon" style (*Charleston Courier*, 22 Sept. 1824; cited in Ravenel, *Architects*, 132, n. 54); in that year, he designed the first Gothic Revival building in South Carolina, St. Peter's Catholic Church, Columbia.

[42] See Appendix I under Lancaster.

[43] Maryland Historical Society, Washington Monument Papers, MS 876, Box I.

[44] Bess Glenn and A.S. Salley, *Some Letters of Robert Mills, Engineer and Architect* (Columbia, 1928), 9. Mills was seeking employment as early as 1826. (*ibid.*, p. 6).

[45] Although Mills's choice of the temple form was probably influenced by Jefferson's Virginia Capitol, he may also have been influenced by Jefferson's designs for the Botetourt Courthouse (c. 1818, but its appearance is not known; Fiske Kimball, *Thomas Jefferson, Architect* . . . [Boston, 1916, 80; hereafter Kimball, *Jefferson*]. Jefferson also designed a courthouse for Birmingham County in 1821 (*ibid.*, 80-81, 192-195; figs. 214-215), a temple-form building with four Tuscan columns supporting a pediment slightly less in height than one-fifth its width. The descriptions of this building indicate that it, like the original designs for the Virginia Capitol, did not have a ground floor. Latrobe, the other major influence on Mills, had not designed a purely temple-form building, and when Latrobe designed a courthouse for Hagerstown, Maryland in 1817, he produced a distinctive form of his own (Hamlin, *Latrobe*, fig. 27; cf. Library of Congress, Mills Papers, MS1386, Box 1, p. 20). For discussion of the relative importance of the influence of Jefferson and Latrobe, see Gene Waddell, "Robert Mills's Fireproof Building," *South Carolina Historical Magazine* vol. 80 (1979), 121-123, (hereafter, Waddell, "Fireproof Building").

A Pre-Revolutionary, temple-form building which may have influenced Mills is Prince William's Parish Church, Beaufort County, South Carolina. Its brickwork pattern incorporates the year 1751, evidently its date of construction, and although it was burned in 1779 and 1865, the ruins have survived largely intact (Samuel Gaillard Stoney, *Plantations of the Carolina Low Country*; ed. by Albert Simons and Samuel Lapham, Jr. [Charleston, 1955 rev.], 173 and 63. This building was described as "almost finished" on 21 April 1753; 4 *Stat.* 3. A painting of c. 1798 shows that it had a four-column portico and thus almost certainly a gable roof (Charles Fraser, *A Charleston Sketchbook*, 1797-1806, with an introduction and notes by Alice R. Huger Smith [Charleston, 1959], pl. 7; Fraser has exaggerated the height of the attic and misplaced the belt course, but all the major elements of the design are present). Mills designed a church of similar size with a temple form for John's Island in c. 1804 (not constructed; Samuel Lapham, Jr., "Architectural Specifications of a Century Ago . . . ," *Architectural Record*, March 1923, 239-244). The drawings and specifications are now in the Charleston Library Society, and their significance is reappraised in a forthcoming article by Rhodri Liscombe, "Robert Mills's Church Architecture."

[46] For example, the Kershaw Courthouse (built 1825-1832; SCDAH mfm 7-8A53 and 7-8B252) cost $9,892 of a $10,000 appropriation (*Acts*, 1823, 118. SCDAH mfm 7-8A53 and 7-8B252; cf. agreement dated 12 May 1825 in Bonds and the CPB petition dated 13 Dec. 1831 with 10-3-n.d. 486-3/6). The identical amount was appropriated for courthouses at Greenville, Newberry, Spartanburg, Union, Williamsburg, York, Georgetown and Lancaster (SCDAH Reports 1821-99 and 1822-110). Williamsburg and Georgetown cost more to complete.

[47] The districts did not have an executive (chairman or manager) or a legislative body (council); decisions ordinarily made by these offices were handled through resolutions (rather than acts) of the Legislature. Most resolutions involving public buildings resulted from petitions by district commissioners of public buildings or contractors and through grand jury presentments. For the development of local government, see Anne King Gregorie, "County Offices" (unpublished summary of relevant legislation prepared for WPA workers. MS, SCHS 28-34-5).

[48] This had been the solution for the Virginia Capitol (although Jefferson had not planned a ground floor), for the east face of U.S. Capitol, and for the South Carolina State

House in Columbia (completed 1790). This solution places the courtroom in the equivalent of a piano nobile and the offices on the service level, the scheme of many Renaissance villas and palaces. Mills's courthouses with attached porticos, his Fireproof Building, his Asylum, and his house for Ainsley Hall so closely resemble several of Jefferson's houses that he was probably influenced by their overall appearance (especially by Poplar Forest) and by Jefferson's predilection for Palladian design.

[49] The 1809 Statute (5 *Stat.* 597) provided fines for encroachment on these public squares. For Darlington, see Fig. 31E and the elaborate notes A. Blanding filed with his letter of 28 June 1822 (SCDAH). The illustration of the Colleton site indicates that its jail was behind and to the right of its courthouse; no streets are evident. The contemporary illustration of the Greenville Courthouse seems to show an open square reserved in front. For an 1823 plan of Newberry, see Fig. 30A herein and Thomas H. Pope, *The History of Newberry County, South Carolina; Volume One: 1749-1860* (Columbia, 1973), 95; the earlier courthouse had been on the same square (Legislative Petition; n.d., but c. 1852. For the plan, see SCDAH Report 1823-171-07). See Appendix I herein for Spartanburg, whose courthouse site was approved by Blanding rather than Mills.

[50] In his design for Kershaw, Mills sacrificed courtroom space for visual effect, and his successors did not approve. When the courthouse was redesigned in the 1840's, the stairs were moved from the vestibule to the outside, and they were placed in front for direct access to the courtroom (as had been done for Edgefield in the 1830's).

[51] See also Robert L. Alexander, *The Architecture of Maximilian Godefroy* (Baltimore, 1974), 126-129.

[52] *Statistics*, 408.

[53] *Ibid.*, 407.

[54] Ottavio Bertotti Scamozzi, *Le Fabbriche e i Disegni de Andrea Palladio* (New York, 1968 reprint of the 1796 Italian ed.), bk. 2, pl. 41. While Mills obviously does not copy this plate, he does reproduce the overall effect, which is achieved by placing a four-columned, monumental portico in the center of a five bay façade and by raising the portico on an arcaded base. In addition to Charleston public buildings that Mills knew well and praised in his *Statistics*, he surely also admired the finest plantation house near Charleston and the finest town house in Charleston, both of which have essentially Palladian main facades and dual entrances that are derived directly or indirectly from plates in the *Four Books*. Drayton Hall (c. 1738) has ground floor entrances on its land and river sides and pair of outside stairs leading to its main floor. The Miles Brewton House has similar ground floor entrances, and the street front has a pair of stairs which lead to each side of its portico. (For his ownership of a French edition of Scamozzi's book, see Gallagher, *Mills*, 24. For his admiration of Palladio, *ibid.*, 154).

Jefferson frequently employed attached porticoes on dwellings in emulation of Palladio, but he preferred to have their stuccoed columns stand out against an unstuccoed brick surface, as at Monticello and also at Poplar Forest, which had an arcaded base; the Virginia Capitol is an exception in having been stuccoed. Most of Mills's South Carolina buildings are stuccoed, but the ones of brick with only the columns stuccoed, such as Bethesda Church, Ainsley Hall's house, and the Horry Courthouse have an even greater resemblance to Jefferson's buildings.

For Mills's comments on the use of books, see Gallagher, *Mills,* 170; he stated that "books are useful to the student, but when he enters upon the practice of his profession, he should lay them aside and only consult them upon doubtful points, or in matters of detail or as mere studies, not to copy buildings from."

The general absence of decorative detail and the general reliance for visual effect on careful proportion may be derived from a statement in Vitruvius, whom Mills called "that great master": "when it appears that a work has been carried out sumptuously, the owner will be the person to be praised for the great outlay which he has authorized; when delicately, the master workman will be approved for his execution; but when proportions and symmetry lend it an imposing effect, then the glory of it will belong to the architect"

(*Ten Books on Architecture,* trans. by Morris Hecky Morgan [New York, 1910], 192; see Gallagher, *Mills,* 154).

[55] Harold Kirker, *The Architecture of Charles Bulfinch* (Cambridge, Mass., 1969), 29-31 (hereafter, Kirker, *Bulfinch*). Another example was his Congregational Church, Pittsfield, Mass., 1790-1793 (*ibid.,* 25-27).

[56] This building was authorized in 1786 and when completed, it had straight steps at each end of its portico (Fig. 51B. 4 *Stat.* 751). On 20 December 1810, the Legislature appropriated funds for erecting a flight of stone steps to the State house . . . " (5 *Stat.* 638), and from the permanency of the material, these were likely the curved stairs which appear in a drawing made between 1858 and 1865, (Christie Zimmerman Fant, *The State House of South Carolina* . . . [Columbia, 1970], 12 and 108). The State House appears to have been the model for Rose Hill Plantation (which had a similar portico and stair arrangement believed to date before 1820; Bilodeau, *Art,* fig. 118) and possibly for the present Marion CH. Mills and Manigault were probably familiar with Government House in New York City and may have adapted its pair of curved stairs at the ends of a tetra-style portico; both had visited New York while this building was still standing (John A. Kouwenhoven, *The Columbia Historical Portrait of New York* . . . [New York . . . , 1972], p. 88, top; Gallagher, *Mills,* p. 8; Manigault Papers, SCHS. The entablature of the Government House portico breaks forward for the space of its central bay in a way which suggests the treatment of the Colleton and Fairfield pediments). The earliest known plan of the White House also shows a pair of curving stairs (south front; Kimball, *Jefferson,* pl. 179).

Multiple entrances are characteristic of Pre-Revolutionary Charleston single houses; one was for business, another for family, and a third for servants.

[57] *Statistics,* 700. Fiske Kimball attributes the State House to Hoban and states that Hoban was influenced by L'Enfant's design for the Federal Hall in New York (*Dictionary of American Biography,* IX, 91).

[58] Kirker, *Bullfinch,* 165-167.

[59] Desmond Guinness and Julius Trousdale Sadler, Jr., *Mr. Jefferson, Architect* (New York, 1973), 156-159.

[60] These 18th Century vaults were much thicker than the ones used by Mills, who "introduced the use of hydraulic cement . . . " (Gallagher, *Mills,* 166; but cf. Hamlin, *Latrobe,* 366, 448n, and 561). Mills's vaulting techniques were criticized unjustly during the 1820's (e.g., fn. 35 herein and the Appendix for Newberry), as they were later to be in his Treasury Building. Three of the vaults for his Newberry Courthouse collapsed during construction because cold weather prevented the cement from setting properly. On the other hand, the vaults of his Fireproof Building survived in 1886 earthquake without any visible cracks. It can also be argued that the man who designed the world's tallest masonry structure was a capable engineer. While Mills undoubtedly made mistakes, any inadequacies in his buildings are less likely to be through errors in design than through errors in construction. (For a completely unjust and virulent criticism of Mills's vaulting techniques by Thomas U. Walter, see William H. Pierson, Jr., *American Buildings and their Architects; the Colonial and Neoclassical Styles* [Garden City, 1970], 415-16; hereafter, Pierson, *American Buildings*).

[61] *The Four Books of Architecture* (New York, 1965 reprint of the 1738 edition), bk. 2, pl. 39. George J. Giger, *A Model Jail of the Olden Time . . . for Burlington . . . , May 1808* (New York, 1928); cf. Gallagher, *Mills,* opp. 24 & 26 (also 200-203). For Latrobe, see William Howard Adams (ed.), *The Eye of Th: Jefferson* (Washington, 1976), Figs. 406-407.

[62] Gallagher, *Mills,* 170.

[63] The Fireproof Building was constructed between May 1822 and December 1826; and although Mills was a member of the local commission in charge of its construction, his designs were significantly altered (Waddell, "Fireproof Building," 105-135) Mills won a nationally advertised design competition for the Asylum (SCDAH, Report 1822-140-07). Construction was begun in July 1822 (*Oration, on the laying of the corner stone of the Lunatic Asylum, at Columbia, S.C. July 1822;* Charleston, 1822). The plan permitted enlargement "without injury to the symmetry and proportions of the building . . . " (*Acts,* 1822, 103-

104) by providing for wings to be added in sections and eventually to form a semicircular court (Mills, *Statistics*, 705). The final appropriation for construction was in December 1826 (*Acts*, 15). For Mills's designs, see Gallagher *Mills*, opp. 50 and 52, and Bryan, *Mills*, 20-21 and items 50-59.

[64] Albert and Harriett Porcher Simons suggested this in an article in *The State and The Columbia Record* (newspaper, 20 October 1963, 16D), and the reason they gave was the equal spacing of the four columns, rather than a wider central bay. Another reason end stairs were likely to have been intended is that at each of its ends, the portico floor is attached to the front wall by an arch which is incorporated into the wall (Fig. 46B), rather than into pilaster-like projections as at each end of the porch on the opposite side of the house. (The 1823 contracts are in the South Caroliniana Library, University of South Carolina; photocopies are in the Papers of Harriett Porcher Stoney Simons, SCHS 26-89. See HABS No. 13-16 for measured drawings.

For the history of the Columbia Academy, see David W. Robinson, "Columbia Academy," an address before the Cosmos Club, 15 November 1977 (typescript in the South Caroliniana Library, University of South Carolina, Columbia; I & O 8612.) A lot was purchased in 1822 (p. 4). An early lithograph in the Caroliniana shows the building in c. 1841 (P/8375; Figure 45 herein). For another similar possibility, see Figure 47B.

[65] The Church was dedicated in October 1822 (Carl Julien and Daniel W. Hollis, *Look to the Rock; One Hundred Ante-bellum Presbyterian Churches of the South* [Richmond 1961]). For a print by J. Hall that is based on a drawing by Mills, see Fig. 44 (Gallagher's reproduction gives the location incorrectly [*Mills*, opp. 86, but correctly on p. 83]); the publication date on this print is 1 September 1827. The attached portico and outside stairs on the back of this church are later additions; to accomodate this stair arrangement, a window was closed and two doors were cut.

[66] The vaulting of the central magazine resembles a Gothic chapter house. These buildings were begun in 1822 (SCDAH, Report, 1822-110) and completed in 1829 (*Acts*, 1828, 12, 43; 1839, 9). The HABS prepared measured drawings of these buildings prior to their demolition (S.C. 13-13). For illustrations, see Ravenel, *Architects*, 129-131.

[67] Library of Congress, Mills Papers, 1368, Box I. Two plans for the Library in the South Caroliniana Library indicate that Mills's building would have had masonry vaults on both floors.

[68] National Archives, Cartographic Department, NSP-0-29130, dated 17 July 1838; illustrated in Gallagher, *Mills*, opp. 56, and herein as Figs. 48-49.

[69] The payment to Elliot is noted in *Receipts and Expenditures of the United States* (Washington, D.C., 1837), 55. For the influence of Davis, see J.B. Davies, "A.J. Davis' Projects for a Patent Office Building, 1832-1834," *JSAH*, 24 (1965), no. 3, 229-251, and Pierson, *American Buildings*, 404-417. For a summary of the documentation, see Louise Hall, "The Design of the Old Patent Office," *JSAH*, vol. XV (March 1956), 27-30; Mills claimed to have designed the exteriors of all three buildings, and his assertions merit further consideration.

The General Post Office was described as being "Italian or Palladian" in style by R.D. Owen in *Hints on Public Architecture* (New York, 1849), 98, although the south facade and especially the side porticos recall William Wilkins' National Gallery and Royal Academy, London, for illustrations of which and the history of its construction, see R[hodri] W[indsor] Liscombe, *William Wilkins, 1778-1839* (Cambridge, 1980), pl. 95 and 180-209.

[70] Of the persons born in South Carolina and living in the United States in 1850, 41 percent had moved to other states; see Tommy W. Rogers, "The Great Population Exodus from South Carolina, 1850-1860," *South Carolina Historical Magazine*, vol. 68 (1967), 16-18.

[71] The drawings are part of the SCHS Mills Papers, 33-22.

[72] This review is based upon the files assembled for the survey of courthouses in the United States published as *Courthouse: A Photographic Document* (see fn. 1 herein) and now in the Prints and Photographs Department, Library of Congress, and upon the HABS.

[73] Illustrated in C.M. Greiff, *Lost America* (New York, 1971), pl. 16.

[74] Wood was used nearly twice as often as brick for the courthouses which had been built before Mills came to South Carolina. Of twenty-one recorded examples, thirteen were wood. Seven were brick, and one (Lexington) had a brick first story and a wooden second story. All six of the courthouses which were to have been built to the designs of William Jay would have had brick walls, but wooden floors. (The sources for information on earlier courthouses are Thomas Baker's 1820 summary and Mills's 1822 summary for the Legislature in the Reports of the BPW for those years; *Improvement*, 25-34, 151-162. Supplemental information is from Mills, *Statistics*.) Mills's courthouses were brick, except for York and Union, which had stone facings; and all of his ground floors had masonry vaults (excluding the redesigned Jay buildings). Five of the seven courthouses designed by others in the 1820's were of brick; one was of stone (Lexington) and one of wood (Pickens). Only one courthouse designed by someone other than Mills, Lancaster, is known to have been built using his vaulting techniques.

The only available illustration of a courthouse built between 1800 and 1820 is the one in the center of Mills's drawing of the Fairfield Courthouse at Winnsboro (Figure 7), and it could be mistaken for a domestic building. Excluding Jay's courthouses, the average number of square feet in fifteen 1800-1820 examples was 3,161; three courthouses by Jay had 4,000; excluding the attached porticoes, three of Mills's courthouses had 4,107, but excluding the integral portico of his Kershaw Courthouse, its area was 4,770 or about a third larger than the early average. Between 1800-1830, no courthouse is known to have had only one story; all were two storied except for the three storied Chesterfield Courthouse. The three storied Charleston Courthouse is not considered because it was originally built as a statehouse, and it served a much greater population than any of the other courthouses; its area was 21,600 square feet.

Five later courthouses (1830-1860) had areas averaging 4,564 (excluding their attached porticoes). Newberry, including its integral portico, had an area of 5,632, comparable in size to the area of Kershaw, which with its portico had approximately 5,597 (not including its additions).

The average area of thirteen earlier jails (excluding one for Pendleton built to Jay's specifications) was 2,765 square feet, and several of these were three storied. Jay's building was 3,150 square feet and two storied. Of seventeen whose number of stories is known, twelve were two storied and five were three storied. Five of Mills's jails, all two storied, averaged 3,613 square feet and so were about one third larger in area. Seven later jails average 4,529 or nearly twice as many square feet as the earlier jails and about half again as many as Mills's jails. Of these seven later jails, five were two storied and two were three storied. The materials used for jails was almost uniformly brick before, during, and after Mills's involvement. Of twenty-one earlier jails, brick was used for eighteen, brick and stone for one, stone only for one, and wood for one. Later jails were generally of brick; eight out of nine examples were brick, and the remaining one (Pickens) was of wood.

[75] Beck had worked on the Ainsley Hall house and on Mills's Laurens J; he designed a jail for Richland (*q.v.* Appendix I). The 1838 agreement is in the SCDAH (and cf. mfm 7-8C55).

[76] The foundation proved insecure (certificate of Thos. L. Sanders, 1 October 1844, SCDAH) through no fault of Mills, who inherited the walls half-built, or Jay, who had specified "piling if necessary." The courthouse was replaced with funds appropriated in 1841: "For the Courthouse of Colleton District, eight thousand dollars, provided the same be built of brick or stone . . . ;" the amount and the choice of materials indicates an entirely new building (11 *Stat.* 149 and in 1822 $400 more, 11 *Stat.* 217). An undated (1842) petition of the CPB states that the former courthouse had deteriorated too much to be sold for any other purpose and that it was turned over to J. & B. Lucas & Dawson to salvage as much of its materials as could be reused for the new courthouse (SCDAH).

A total of $8,500 was appropriated for the courthouse, $8,000 in December, 1841 and $500 in December 1842 (11 *Stat.* 149, 217). J & B Lucas & Dawson received payments of $2,666.66 on 16 May and 7 November 1842 and in April 1843, representing the beginning, mid-point, and end of construction; an extra payment of $500 was made 10 May 1843 (SCDAH, mfm 7-2E, 227, 245, 255, and 257).

[77] A copy of a photograph is in the Abbeville County Museum, which occupies a three-story brick jail that is considered to have been "Designed by Robert Mills 1830" (from a sign in front). This building was built with appropriations made in December 1852 and December 1853. The Abbeville Commissioners of Public Buildings in an undated petition (which from internal evidence was submitted in 1853) stated that the former jail had been standing at least fifty years. The new jail was to be built "to a plan and specifications made by the architect J. Graves." (For the appropriation see 12 *Stat.* 131.)

[78] See Appendix I for Barnwell. The Berkeley County Courthouse, built in 1885 and now the town hall for Mt. Pleasant, has dual entrances (dated in an article by Bob Stockton, *News and Courier*, 16 Jan. 1974.)

[79] *Art Work of Columbia, S.C.* Published in Nine Parts by the Gravure Illustration Co. (n.p., 1905), part 4, no. 3. Figure 58B herein.

"In 1953 the Williamsburg County Board of Supervisors made their courthouse even more characteristic of Mills than before" (W.G. Barner in *The News and Courier*, 22 April 1956).

For Aiken, see the National Register of Historic Places Inventory — Nomination (copy in SCHS, 30-8-61). The c. 1881 courthouse was designed by R.W. McGrath and was re-designed in 1934 by an Augusta, Ga., architect, Willis Irvin.

[80] The five arches (four of them false) give this building an even closer resemblance to Thornton's design for Pavillion VII of the University of Virginia than to Mills's designs. The stair solution of straight flights at each end of the portico was one which Mills had not used. (For biographical information on White and illustrations of buildings by him, see Ravenel, *Architects*, 183-202.)

[81] Ravenel, *Architects*, 186, 195, 199. For Strickland's original design, see Charles Fraser, *An Address . . . at the Laying of the Corner Stone of a New College Edifice . . ., on the 12th of January, 1828* (Charleston, 1828), frontispiece.

[82] Letter to his wife, Eliza Barnwell Smith Mills, dated 30 September 1827; Mills Papers, SCHS 11-517.

APPENDIX I

SOUTH CAROLINA COURT HOUSES AND JAILS OF THE 1820s

Abbeville

The contract for the Abbeville courthouse states that it is to be built "in all respects according to the plan and specifications made out by Robert Mills." Campbell Humphrys, the contractor, agreed on 13 May 1828 to complete construction by the third Monday in Oct. 1829 (SCDAH, Bonds). For a new courthouse and for repairs to the existing jail, the Legislature had appropriated $9,500 in Dec. 1827 to be added to $500 appropriated in its previous session. (*Acts*, 1827-1828, 11). Treasury payments indicate that an advance of one-third of the total was paid on 22 May 1828; the walls were up by 3 Oct.; the building was received and final payment was made 24 March, 1830 (SCDAH mfm 7-8A215 and 7-8B187). An agreement of 18 Nov. 1828 specified $842.87½ for additional work, including rusticated stone for the lower story, a stone belt course, and stone arches for the portico. James H. Tusten agreed 4 Nov. 1828 to make the necessary jail repairs for $550 by the third Monday of Mar. 1829; consequently a new jail was not needed. In a contract dated 14 Mar. 1829, Timothy D. Williams agreed to paint the exterior walls of the courthouse with two coats of Venetian red and to paint the roof of the main block and of the portico "a good slate color." The fragmentary descriptions indicate that the courthouse had an attached portico with columns on an arcaded basement (cf. SCDAH contract for ironwork, 9 April 1832).

Mills's CH replaced a brick one built in 1810 (SCDAH 7-1B100 and 5 *Stat.* 616, 692); it was two-storied, 60' x 40' (*Improvement*, 25). A three-story brick J (37' x 28') had been built in 1802-1803 and was repaired; it did not need replacing (SCDAH mfm 7-1B100; *Improvement*, 25, 110). Mills's CH and the old J were both replaced with appropriations of 1852-1853 (12 *Stat.* 131, 202). See also Bernard and Kay C. Bydalek, "The Courthouses at Abbeville," *Historic Courthouses of South Carolina: Abbeville* (Columbia, 1980).

The entry for this CH indicates the types of information that are available for further study of individual courthouses and jails. Subsequent entries deal primarily with whether or not Mills was involved in the design and with how his buildings were altered.

Anderson

The Anderson CH was probably based on plans by Mills, but the specifications have features which indicate that they were prepared by someone else. The Anderson specifications were agreed to by Benajah Dunham on 12 April 1827, and they were adapted from specifications for a CH which was to have been built for Pendleton District (*q.v.*; the Pendleton CH was not built when the Legislature decided to abolish Pendleton District and to divide its territory into Anderson and Pickens Districts [*Acts*, 1826, 38-40; 1827, 33-34 and 66-70]).

Mills in his *Statistics* (674) noted that "a new courthouse on an elegant and spacious plan will soon be erected here," implying that the design was his. The agreement calls for a two-story brick building with offices below; courtroom above; a tetrastyle, attached portico with a pair of curving stairs; however, the offices were not to be fireproofed. Although the Greenville CH (*q.v.*; by Mills) is referred to as a possible model for doors, an alternative suggestion was "Figure I. Plate 30. in [Asher] Benjamins Architecture . . . ," a suggestion Mills would not have made. The new contract with Dunham included most of the same specifications as for Pendleton (and frequently the same unusual phrasing, but not the references to door models); it called for completion by 25 May 1829. The walls were up by 22 Nov. 1827 (SCDAH, 10-4-1827-133-5), indicating that the deadline was probably met. The total of the contract was $8,400, and the dimensions are given as 42' x 48' (and 30' high). An early drawing of the courthouse shows that it closely resembled the Marlborough prototype (Robert Eflin, Harold Cooledge, and Donald Collins, *Anderson Historic District Study*, 1974, [n.p., n.d.], cover illustration). This drawing also shows a J with two stories, a three-bay front, and end chimneys, features shared by the Colleton J. Fig. 30C herein.

The CH was remodeled and enlarged with an 1852 appropriation (12 *Stat.* 131); it was destroyed to provide a site for another CH that was completed in 1898 (Louise Ayer Vandiver, *Traditions and History of Anderson County* [Atlanta, 1928], 277-278). The J was replaced with an appropriation of 1849 (11 *Stat.* 555).

Barnwell

A wooden courthouse for Barnwell had been completed before Mills returned to South Carolina. An act of 1816 provided $6,000 for a building 50' x 40' (x 35' to the eaves), to be completed by November 1819 (which was accomplished; *Improvement*, A3, 2). As one of the last public buildings erected without a professional architect's designs, its deficiencies deserve notice: The courtroom was in the first story and was adjacent to the public square; noise from outside and from the offices and jury rooms upstairs caused frequent interruptions in courtroom business. The offices above could only be entered by a staircase "which runs its whole length up through the courtroom, starting from near the Judges Seat." The building was not fireproof and in an emergency, records could not be removed quickly. (Petition of A.P. Aldrich, 18 Nov. 1844). The earlier two-story brick J was repaired (SCDAH mfm 7-7C97).

Another CH was not authorized until 1844 (11 *Stat.* 289; specifications in the SCDAH dated 25 March 1845 indicate that on its south face it had a tetrastyle portico and a pair of curving stairs between the outside inter-columnations and rising to a platform which was between the two inner columns. The order was "Grecian Ionic.") On its north face, it had an attached tetrastyle portico. That CH was burned in 1865 (13 *Stat.* 244). The present CH shows strong influence by Mills, but was built in 1878-1879 (Emily Bellinger Reynolds and Joan Reynolds Faunt, *The County Offices and Officers of Barnwell County, S.C., 1775-1975*, [Columbia 1976], 111). A new J was not contracted for until 6 June 1833, so neither of this district's buildings were by Mills.

Beaufort (Coosawhatchie)

The site of the CH was moved from the town of Beaufort to the more central location of Coosawhatchie in 1788 (5 *Stat.* 76). On 18 December 1817, an appropriation of $12,000 was for a new CH & J (6 *Stat.* 87), but this amount proved insufficient (*Improvement*, A2). A year later, in December 1818, $2,400 more was to be used for these buildings and, if needed, an additional $600 for two lots. Construction had not begun at the beginning of 1819, but it was nearly complete at the end of 1820 (*ibid.*, 1-2, 26-27, 110). Surviving plans (SCDAH, MF 17-17; Figs. 2-3 herein) are almost certainly by Jay, primarily because they resemble his standard design that was used for the Sumter CH, as is discussed in the text. Mills described the Beaufort buildings as "a neat substantial brick court-house and jail . . . " (*Statistics*, 368). The site of the CH was moved to Gillisonville by an act of 21 December 1836, and both Coosawhatchie buildings were sold (petition, CPB, 1 November 1841).

Charleston

The Charleston CH was repaired in 1819, 1825, and 1826 (SCDAH mfm, 7-1B272, 427) and has survived; Mills had no opportunity to replace it. The J also did not need to be replaced, but it required enlargement; and Mills designed a four-story fireproof wing, as has been mentioned in the text (*Improvement*, 151). Appropriations for an entirely new jail were authorized in 1853 and 1854 (12 *Stat.* 202, 276). See Robert P. Stockton, "Jail's Octagonal Wing Miscredited to Mills," *The News and Courier*, 23 Jan. 1978; also, Fig. 30B herein.

Chester (Chesterville)

An appropriation of $6,000 made in Dec. 1818 was inadequate for a CH so $3,000 was added in Dec. 1819 (*Improvement*, A6, 3). Work had then been delayed until Jay joined the BPW. A total of $6,000 had been paid by 13 Dec. 1820, probably indicating that the walls at least had been completed before Mills joined the BPW (*ibid.*, 158. This is also likely because the courtroom was in the first story (Petition, CPB, n.d., [c. 1849], requesting a new CH]). By Dec. 1821, the CH was considered completed (*Improvement*, 111). During 1821 and 1822, an additional $4,332 was paid out. In a subsequent, undated petition after completion, the contractor, William Turner, stated that "several changes were made by authority of Captain Baker" and that the overall costs were far greater than anticipated because in order to complete the work within the time stipulated in his contract, he had been forced to employ workmen at wages "raised to a very high rate" by numerous other state-sponsored public works (SCDAH, 10-3-ND-521 and cf. 527). He does not mention Mills, and he would surely have done so if he could have blamed him for increasing the costs. Although Mills referred to the CH and J as "handsome" (*Statistics*, 492), he also praised the Beaufort CH; Chester too was likely to be by Jay. Funds for the present CH were appropriated in 1850 (12 *Stat.* 8), and it was built "according to plans and specifications made and drawn by Edward B. White Architect of Charleston, dated the 8 day of April A.D. 1852 . . . ," plans which, as noted, are indebted to Mills. The old CH was sold and the new one had been completed by 1824 (SCDAH, Petition, n.d.; approved 21 Dec. 1854).

A contract for the J was signed 23 Jan. 1818 and Stephen Terry, its contractor, was advanced 60 percent of the $5,000 appropriation on that date. He did not receive the first payment until 19 March 1822 (*Improvement*, 160). By Dec. 1820, little had been done beyond the collection of some material. Although Mills could have redesigned the J, he probably did not because Terry also does not mention changes in an elaborate justification for additional expense (SCDAH, 10-3-NC-527). Instead, Terry appealed for compensation primarily on the basis of an underestimate because of his inexperience. A letter from Chesterville dated 21 December 1822 does mention that the roof was left unpainted ". . . in as much as it was stated by Mr. Mills that the painting of the roof, was rather an injury, than an advantage . . . " (signature illegible). The J was replaced with an appropriation of 1839 (11 *Stat.* 100).

Chesterfield

Since the 7 March 1825 specifications refer to Mills's plans and since the contractor, John Chapman, Jr., blamed Mills for deficiencies in the plans (10-3-ND-433), there can be no doubt that he provided the atypical design for the CH. The building was received 29 October 1827 and additional expenditures were listed and approved (SCDAH, Bonds; mfm 7-8A51. See Appendix II, item 6 herein). It was burned in 1865 (13 *Stat.* 243-244), but is illustrated in the *Harper's Weekly* issue for 1 April 1865 (from a sketch made 2 Mar., showing that the roof had been altered during construction from a low hip to gabled ends; the stairs were built straight along the face of the building).

The existing J was repaired (*Improvement*, 110) and served until 1842 (4 *Stat.* 612 for 1838 appropriation; SCDAH letter of 21 Sept. 1842).

Colleton (Walterborough)

The CH designed by Jay and redesigned by Mills is considered in the text and its replacement is considered in footnote 76. The redesigned J was replaced with an appropriation of 1853 (12 *Stat.* 202).

Darlington

A Darlington CH can be attributed to Mills because an appropriation was approved for it at the end of his year as SPB ($10,000; *Acts*, 1823, 118). It was built between 1824 and

1826 (SCDAH mfm 7-7C97 and 7-8A215). It was enlarged with an appropriation of 1853 (12 *Stat.* 202); a contract with R.F. Ligon dated 23 June 1854 includes plans showing that jury rooms and stairs were added above to the back with more offices below; and a rear elevation shows a three-bay, pedimented end; the contract states that ". . . the new building when finished to present externally the appearance of old building" (Figs. 32B & 33). Gen. Joseph Burch Nettles in 1879 stated that "the Court House which was destroyed by fire in 1866, was built by General Evander R. McIver in 1825-26," (quoted in Eliza Cowan Ervin and Horace Fraser Rudisill, *Darlingtoniana* . . . , [Columbia, 1964] 12-13, 19, 24; Anne King Gregorie cites a tablet in a later CH as providing 25 March 1866 for the date of the fire and 1870 as the date it was rebuilt [SCHS MS 28-35-5-32]. A photograph of c. 1880 in Ervin and Rudisill's book shows that the rebuilt CH resembled the Horry CH in its design. The original walls and portico were evidently reused, judging from the resemblance to an early wood engraving in *Harper's Weekly*, 30 Sept. 1865, 615 (called to our attention by Mr. Rudisill).

The existing J was repaired (*Improvement*, 150-151; SCDAH mfm 7-7C96) and sufficed until it was replaced with appropriations of 1837 and 1839 (4 *Stat.* 591; 11 *Stat.* 7).

Edgefield

Although its CH was considered "a slight, rough, inferior building" in 1820, it was relatively large, of brick, and capable of repair (*Improvement*, 28, 120). Identical porticos with pairs of stairs were added to the east and west fronts, and extensive remodeling was specified in a contract dated 20 July 1827 (7-8A 289); Mills obviously did not prepare the specifications. The existing courthouse with strong Mills influence was not built until 1838-1839 (SCDAH mfm 7-8C55; agreement, Bonds, 7 May 1838).

A new J was recommended by Thomas Baker in 1820: "When examining these cells, the heat and stench about them were so great that I was obliged to decline entering. Those confined in them are always shrouded in darkness . . . Any confinement in this gaol, is an excessive punishment, and if long continued, must prove fatal to the unfortunate person subject to it" (*Improvement*, 28). A new J after a Mills design was built for $8,000 in 1825 (SCDAH mfm 7-8A47); the agreement signed by Campbell Humphries of Union District states that it was to be completed "in every particular and after the model of the Union jail . . . " by 1 March 1826. A petition for an additional $600 to face the front with stone "hewed smooth instead of being put up in a rough state" was denied, even though the CPW was "persuaded that it would add greatly to the strength, beauty and durability of the said building . . . " (n.d.). It was replaced with appropriations of 1850 and 1852 (12 *Stat.* 8, 131.)

Fairfield (Winnsborough)

Mills redesigned the Jay CH under construction (as is discussed in the text). The CH was enlarged and a portico was added with an appropriation of 1843 (11 *Stat.* 253; the appropriation was preceded by a series of petitions which speculated on Mills's intentions). The agreement is dated 20 April 1841 and includes the specifications that an addition of 16' is to be added to the back and a 14' wide portico is "to extend the whole length of the old building . . . " (which had been built broader than it was deep). The first story of the portico was to have piers and the second story four columns supporting a "full Tuscan Cornice." A pair of L-shaped stairs were within the portico (rather than at the ends as with Mills's CH's or in front as in some CH's based on Mills's plans). The existing stairs which wind between the end intercolumniations date from 1939 (Cf. Fig. 8B & 9B). The J was repaired (*Improvement*, 111) and was not replaced until after an appropriation of 1835 (4 *Stat.* 546; an agreement dated 9 May 1837 includes plans that were realized in 1837-1838 [SCDAH mfm 7-8C52]).

Georgetown

Funds for a new CH were approved in December 1822 ($12,000; *Acts*, 102) so there can be little doubt that the design was furnished by Mills and not by Russell Warren, despite a *Georgetown Gazette* article of November 1824 which refers to "Major Warren, the architect who built our courthouse . . . " and despite his design work elsewhere. Warren was contractor for this building and subcontractor for the Horry CH. (Warren was paid for the construction of the Georgetown CH in May 1824 [SCDAH, General Assembly Accounts – Public Works, undated, 1800-1830, VI/22/3/7; folder 1 for 1825]). A payment of $75 was made in 1823 to "E.R. McIver, sup. intd. pub. buildgs., for drawings of Court House" and this payment indicates that he received the fee for someone else (his salary would have covered furnishing plans, as Mills's had when he was SPB). The attribution of the plans to Mills is also based on other considerations besides the fact that the plans were prepared before the 1822 appropriation was made (and thus while he was on the BPW). The building resembles his Williamsburg CH, which was designed in 1821 (in its hexastyle, temple form and similar stair solution. Warren was not involved in this building, and Warren's work was less Palladian and more archaeologically correct in its handling of classical details (cf. Robert L. Alexander, "The Architecture of Russell Warren [thesis, New York University, 1952; SCHS microfiche]). The CH was enlarged with an appropriation at 1853 (12 *Stat.* 202) to the designs of the Charleston architect George E. Walker (Ravenel, *Architects*, 125). The first and second story entrances appear to have been embellished at this time. The existing jail (1811-1812; SCDAH mfm 7-1B133) continued to be used until it was replaced by one authorized in 1841 (11 *Stat.* 149; contract with dated 10 May 1843; cf. petition of Eleazor Waterman, 1 December 1845).

Greenville

The CH plans were probably prepared by Mills in 1821, the year an appropriation was made (*Improvement*, 149; cf. SCDAH 10-4-1822-110) and the first year he was a member of the BPW. The contract is dated 22 April 1822 and the work was completed 12 June 1824. (10-3-1825-46; same, 10-3-ND-478). The walls were partly built twice, but pulled down and rebuilt. The contractors, Isaac P. Pond, Daniel Graham, and Charles McCulloch requested "a reasonable sum for sundry items of work and materials which were ordered by Mr. Mills for the Board of Public Works, and afterward by Mr. McIver Superintendant of Public Buildings . . . " (*ibid.*) An attribution to Mills is safe not only because of the date, but because of several unusual features, including his curving stair solution with a railing only on the outside (as in his drawing of the Fireproof Building; Figure 40 herein; the original building (Fig. 16) also closely resembled his courthouses of the Marlborough type until it was renovated. A petition from the local chairman of the CPB dated 2 December 1851 states that the CH was "dangerous to occupy" and requests an appropriation for a new CH. The Legislature appropriated $8,000 and gave permission to sell the old CH and to apply the funds for the new one. Appropriations of 1851 and 1855 (12 *Stat.* 73, 349f) provided for a replacement in the Gothic style built "according to the plans specifications and drawings of the same made by Jones and Lee architects. . ." (contract with brickmason Alberto E. Burgess dated 1 May 1854; cf. also petition, CPB, 1 Dec. 1855. Cf. Ravenel, *Architects*, 203-230 for information on the Charleston architects Edward C. Jones and Francis D. Lee). Despite the supposedly deteriorated condition in 1851, the Mills courthouse survived as the "Record Building" until 1924 (outlasting the Jones and Lee building, which was demolished in 1915; for illustrations of both, Laura Smith Ebaugh, *Bridging the Gap* [Greenville, 1966], 54-55). In the late 19th century, the Mills courthouse was renovated (Figs. 17 & 18A).

The J was also replaced by one of Mills's designs. A contract with James Bennie, dated 14 May 1828, stipulates that it was to be a slightly modified version of the Laurens J, the specifications of which were attached. It was built of stone in 1829-1830 (SCDAH mfm 7-8B188), and it survived until about 1900 (S.S. Crittenden, *The Greenville Century Book* . . . [Greenville, 1903], 20).

Horry (Conwayborough)

The design for the Horry CH must have been prepared by Mills in 1823 because an appropriation of $10,000 was approved for it at the end of that year, and he was then SPB (*Acts*, 118). The basic form of the building follows his Marlborough plan and had vaulted rooms on the first storey. "Russel Warren" received an initial payment of $5,000 in June 1824, and payment was made for the work accepted in July 1825 (SCDAH mfm 7-1B414). See Appendix II for the specifications which give Warren freedom to redesign the portico and steps. Additional information on Horry district buildings from 1802-1851 is in the "Commissioners Book — Public Buildings" (WPA Project 65-33-118; typescript in SCDAH).

A new J was begun the month that the CH was completed (SCDAH contract dated 9 July; for payment SCDAH mfm 7-1B415) and it in turn was to be completed by 1 March 1827 (for extra payment, cf. *Acts* 1828, 58). In 1823 $3,000 had been appropriated to repair the old jail; when reparing it proved undesirable, an additional $5,000 was appropriated in 1824 for a new building. Although Mills could have designed it, there is no documentary evidence that he did. (For a building that was considered to date from the period of the CH, cf. *Horry County Survey of Historic Places, April 1973* [n.p., n.d.], Fig. 82.)

Kershaw (Camden)

The CH is discussed in the text and was unquestionably designed by Mills. It was begun by Wm. Robinson, carpenter and contractor, in 1825 (SCDAH, agreement 12 May, advance 11 July [mfm 7-8A53], and received 11 December 1830 [mfm 7-8B-252]). The earlier CH was "little more than a frame weatherboarded," and all offices were elsewhere (*Improvement*, 30). In a petition dated 23 Oct. 1845, the Bar of Kershaw proposed additions to the Mills CH, and on 5 Dec. 1845, the CPB complained that renovations were needed similar to those already granted to Fairfield and Sumter and that, regardless, less had been spent initially on Kershaw than for Lancaster and other districts. The Legislature granted a requested $4,000 (11 *Stat.* 315; this had been the same amount appropriated for Fairfield two years earlier), and Kershaw proceeded to add to the back and to update the entire building with the Doric order (which necessitated raising the roof structure in order to accommodate the wider entablature. The six Ionic columns were replaced with four Doric columns, and exterior stairs were run straight down from the center of a second story porch; see the analysis of Henry Boykin, A.I.A., in Gail Moore Morrison and Letitia Allen "Camden and Kershaw County's Courthouses," *Historic Courthouses of South Carolina: Kerhsaw County* [Columbia, 1980], 16).

Funds for a new J were appropriated in 1830 (4 *Stat.* 427; the contract dated 1 Sept. 1832 has plans and specifications which do not resemble Mills's work).

Lancaster

An appropriation of 1825 provided $10,000 for a new CH (4 *Stat.* 281). The existing building has Mills's usual groundfloor arrangement with a central barrel-vaulted hall and flanking offices with cross-vaulting, and the plan with the entrance on a longer side resembles his Chesterfield Courthouse. The original specifications dated 5 May 1826 are in the distinctive handwriting of the contractor, Willis W. Alsobrook, and the structure was built in conformity to them (SCDAH, Petition, n.d. 486-3/6). As completed, the exterior contains a number of features that are unlikely to have been used by Mills in 1826, including modillions and a roof with a standard pitch (rather than one influenced by the Classic Revival). The building had been completed by 10 Sept. 1828 (SCDAH mfm 7-8A216). When Alsobrook attempted to justify spending $3,840.50 more than he was authorized for the building, he blamed the Commissioners for alterations, but did not use the common excuse that an architect had omitted essential requirements (SCDAH, Petition, n.d. 486-3/6, 13/16; cf. 4 *Stat.* 380; *Acts*, 1828, 22; SCDAH, Report, 1828-92). No available evidence suggests, as an historical marker states, that Mills designed this courthouse.

A new J was approved late in 1821, indicating that Mills had prepared the design during his first year on the BPW. An agreement dated 4 July 1822 refers to "the plans and specifications signed by Robert Mills" and the agreement itself is signed by him and by Willis W. Alsobrook, who did only the carpentry (South Caroliniana Library, University of South Carolina, Columbia, MS 3011; *Improvement*, 153, indicated that Gilmor and Thompson contracted separately for the masonry. See fn. 27).

Laurens (Laurensville)

A new CH and J had been approved for Laurens in 1815 (*Acts*, 92) but the $5,000 appropriated was insufficient for the CH alone, and $3,000 more was appropriated to reimburse the contractor, George Grace, in 1818 (*Acts*, 81). The building was thus completed early enough to make any involvement by Mills or Jay in the design unlikely, and its dimensions do not correspond with the sizes they used (*Improvement*, 30).

The J was extensively repaired in 1818 (SCDAH mfm 7-7B101) and was not replaced until 1828 (after more than 2 years of construction; *ibid.*, 7-8A49). Campbell Humphries agreed on 20 February 1827 to build a J using specifications which are nearly identical to four other J's including Union (SCDAH, Bonds).

Lexington

A new CH and J were begun in 1819 by the SPW and the construction was completed by December 1820, when Mills came onto the BPW (*Improvement*, 4; SCDAH mfm 7-7B130). The specifications dated 15 July 1819 called for a CH with a brick first story and a wooden second story, a combination which neither Mills nor Jay used for their courthouses. The J proved unsatisfactory and funds for another one were authorized at the end of 1829 (4 *Stat.* 407 & cf. 591; SCDAH mfm 7-8C129). Although Mills was uninvolved in all four of these buildings, the second CH showed his influence because its specifications call for a portico with "winding steps" (SCDAH; dated 4 Dec. 1838).

Marion

The Legislature appropriated $10,000 for a new CH in 1822 (*Acts*, 93, 102) and $8,000 for a new J in 1823 (*Acts*, 118) so both of these buildings were probably designed by Mills. The CH payments date between Mar. 1823 and May 1825 (SCDAH mfm 7-7C95 and 7-1B413), and the J payments between Apr. 1824 and Mar. 1826 (*ibid.*, 7-1B416). A replacement for the J was approved in 1847 (11 *Stat.* 432, 555) and for the CH in 1851 (the existing CH, which shows Mills's influence in the form of its portico; 12 *Stat.* 73, 131).

Marlborough (Bennettsville)

Most of the work on a new CH and J was completed during 1822 and 1823, with a smaller amount being done in 1824 and still smaller amounts in 1828 and 1829 (SCDAH mfm 7-7C91 and 7-8A292). These buildings were to be prototypes, and numerous CH's were built on a similar plan except that later J's were usually not fireproof. Funds for another J were approved in 1839 and 1840 (4 *Stat.* 612; 11 *Stat.* 7; SCDAH mfm 7-8C142, 167) and for a Gothic CH by Edward C. Jones in 1849 and 1851 (11 *Stat.* 555 and 12 *Stat.* 73; SCDAH, agreement dated 18 Nov. 1850 and CH shown in *Frank Leslie's Illustrated Newspaper*, 8 Apr. 1865). The J was to have had cross vaults, but this specification was eliminated (SCDAH, Proceedings, CPB, fall term 1838 - 1 October 1839; 31 May and 10 June 1839).

Newberry

The initial payment for a new CH was on 10 Apr. 1822 indicating that plans were approved late in 1821; Mills probably prepared the designs during his first year on the BPW. Grafton and Beck continued through 1824 (SCDAH mfm 7-7C92; *Improvement*, 154). A new J was constructed between 9 May 1826 and 15 Jan. 1827 by Campbell Humphries "upon a similar plan & in all respects similar to the present goal at Edgefield Courthouse (except that the front is not to be built of nicely polished Rock)" (SCDAH, agreement dated 1 Apr. 1826). The CH later developed serious cracks and had to be taken down; the CPB attributed the problem to the vaulting and noted that some of it gave way during construction. "They have been informed that the Legislature have made appropriations recently, in cases not nearly so urgent, or necessary as that now asked . . . " (SCDAH, undated peition; 1847). In response to these assertions, the legislative Committee of Public Buildings reported their belief that such defects were attributable "in great measure from the Commissioners of Public Buildings in the several districts not giving to erection of the buildings that close and particular supervision the public interest required." Since an architect had stated that repairs could be made, this Committee recommended that the District pay for them (as provided for in 4 *Stat.* 321, recognized in 4 *Stat.* 578, and reiterated in an act passed 17 December 1841). The CPB did nothing, allowing the deterioration to increase beyond repair and thus making them eligible for state funds to erect a new building. The CPB stated on 25 November 1848 that the fault was probably caused by the method of construction, the unusually severe weather during construction, and an inadequate foundation. They noted that the roof had been raised and joists had been inserted in place of "the original construction [in which] the roof rested on an arch as in the lower story . . . " (confirmed by Carwile's description, which refers to a "vaulted" ceiling, "the points of the arches supported in part by two tall Tuscan columns standing equi-distant between the centre and the side-walls of the room"). In a third petition (undated, but 1849) the CPB gave the opinion of the engineer for a local railroad that the building was beyond repair and added that "the sum asked for by your memorialists, they believe has been heretofore always granted where it has been necessary to erect a new building." After three tries, the Legislature gave in and made appropriations for a new CH (11 *Stat.* 555, 12 *Stat.* 73. Jacob Graves furnished plans and specifications for a Greek Doric hexastyle, temple-form building which survives; SCDAH, Petition, CPB, n.d. [1851]). Once successful, the CPB also requested and received funds for a new J (12 *Stat.* 131, 202).

Orangeburg

A new CH and J were constructed at the same time between 1826 and 1828 (SCDAH mfm 7-8A217; *Acts*, 1825, 11). The agreement dated 19 Mar. 1826 calls William Gray and Joseph B. Dane "architects" and states that the buildings are to be constructed "according to plans and draughts . . . furnished by" them. The specifications indicate that the form followed Mills's Marlborough prototype (including a fireproof ground floor) and a drawing of the CH in the issue of *Frank Leslie's Illustrated News* for 8 Apr. 1865 shows the same features. A petition of the CPB dated 17 Nov. 1827 recommends the addition of a partition that had not been in "the plans of Mr. Mills" (SCDAH 10-4-1827-112). A letter of T.J. Withers to L.M. Keitt dated 1 Dec. 1853 calls this building "one of that batch of courthouses constructed, and ruined in the construction, by Robert Mills, Architect;" (however, he was willing to admit that a "commodious, wholesome" courtroom could be made if the state paid for alterations like those at Kershaw and Sumter; SCDAH. Cf. 12 *Stat.* 131).

These references indicate that Mills probably supplied Gray and Dane with the plans that they were required to "furnish" (that is, pay for out of the contract price). The CH was burned in 1865 (13 *Stat.* 244). The specifications for the jail do not correspond to the Union or Lancaster types, but Mills presumably provided plans for this building also. The J was replaced by a Gothic building which has survived (contract 20 Oct. 1858 with John Lucas, contractor; also illustrated in *Leslie's*).

Pendleton

An existing CH was extensively repaired in 1819 and 1820 (SCDAH mfm 7-7B132 and cf. 7-7C90; *Improvement*, 3, 31-32, 115) and was considered in "complete order" in 1820. Nonetheless, a $10,000 appropriation for a new CH was made in 1825 (*Acts*, 12), one year before this district was abolished by its division into Anderson and Pickens Districts (q.v.; Acts, 1826, 38-40). The specifications are dated 26 April 1826 (SCDAH); and although they have many features not used by Mills, they call for a version of his Marlborough plan. The specifications include the then usual stipulation that one-third of the appropriated amount would be paid in advance to provide materials and begin construction, an additional third upon completing half the construction, and the final third when the building was received. The first third was paid on 3 June 1826 (SCDAH mfm 7-8A 218). In Dec. 1826, the CH was ordered to "be abandoned" after satisfying the contractor for damages, and the remainder of the appropriation was to be combined with an amount to be derived from the sale of materials and to be divided between the two new districts. (Acts, 1826, 89; Acts, 1827, 33 directed that the bricks be sold; cf. also ibid., 40, directing eventual sale of the Pendleton public buildings and a lot; the contract with John S. Allen is dated 26 April 1826 [SCDAH]. Farmers Hall has been confused with this building, but its dimensions are too different for it to be the renovated courthouse [cf. the specifications in SCDAH, Bonds, with HABS Survey S.C. 13-12].)

The J had needed replacing, and a contract was made in 1819, but the contractor, James Hodge, spent the $3,000 advance without accomplishing any work (Improvement, 31-32; SCDAH, Petition, 10-3-1821-49. George Grace, who was surety, undertook the construction at his own expense and performed it so well that he was later reimbursed for his loss. For the additional amount appropriated for Grace, Acts, 1821, 73 and 1822, opp. 70). Although the completion of the J was delayed until 1821, Mills's first year on the BPW, the facade of the existing building conforms closely to Jay's rendering, and Mills evidently did not redesign it. (SCDAH mfm 7-7B129; cf. 7-7C-91; Improvement, 112, 115.) The plans and specifications are dated 1 June 1819, nearly a year before Jay was paid for producing his stock designs, but they are in the same style and hand and can be attributed to him with a fair degree of certainty (SCDAH, Public Improvement Files, 1800-1830, 103-17, 24). For an illustration of the renovated building, Pendleton District Historical and Recreational Commission, Pendleton Historic District, A Survey (Pendleton, 1973), 33.

Pickens

A CH and J were built for this newly created district in 1827-1828 (SCDAH mfm 7-8A290, 292; cf. Pendleton). Both were wooden and are unlikely to have involved Mills (cf. two undated SCDAH petitions of 1849 and 1852 [dates for appropriations in response to them]). The courtroom was on the ground floor until later renovations included digging away the hill on which it was built and placing fireproof offices underneath. Porticoes were also added later expressly to bring the building into fashion. For information about a relatively inexpensive wooden J, which burned when almost completed and which was rebuilt of wood, see SCDAH 10-3-1830-92.

Richland (Columbia)

In the early 1820's the CH and J were in repair (Improvement, 120), but the J was considered too small. A new J was not built until 1829-1830 (SCDAH mfm 7-8B188), when $10,000 was expended. The agreement is dated 18 Mar. 1829 and stipulates that the work was to be done "according to the plan and specifications, drawn and signed by the said Charles Beck (who had worked on Mills's Laurens J and on his house for Ainsley Hall. The specifications for Richland are less detailed and are likely to be by Beck). The Richland CH was replaced with an appropriation of 1858 (12 Stat. 588), and the new CH was burned during the destruction of Columbia.

Spartanburg

A $10,000 appropriation was made for a new CH in 1825 (Acts, 12) and the building was constructed between 7 Oct. 1826 and 2 Oct. 1827 (SCDAH mfm 7-8A218). The specifications are dated 12 August 1826 and call for a building 52' x 42' to be fronted by an attached, arcaded, tetrastyle portico with piers indicated beneath each column and with a ground floor plan similar to [Mills's] Greenville CH; however, "substantial timbers" were to support a brick second floor "instead of arches." The courtroom, jury rooms and trim were to be finished "upon the plan of [Mills's] Union courthouse." These references and descriptions in the specifications of other work to be done (instead of the usual references to accompanying drawings) imply that Mills did not furnish a design. The completed building resembled his work, but was probably not by him. Appropriations for another CH were made in 1855 and 1856 (12 *Stat.* 349f, 420. Specifications dated 1 Aug. 1857 mention "the working plans referred to above drawn by Messrs. Graves, Veal, and Bost" and a Doric entablature for this later building, which is incorrectly attributed to Mills [in Marsh, *Mills,* 149]; this temple-form building nevertheless showed his influence in having had exterior stairs leading to a second story courtroom).

A jail had been built in 1823 (SCDAH mfm. 7-7B93; *Acts,* 1822, 102; SCDAH 10-4-1822-110). The plan was probably prepared in 1822 and so can be attributed to Mills (despite Blanding's having made the final site selection; SCDAH letter to him from CPB, 30 Aug. 1822). Mills describes it as "a handsome and substantial jail, built of granite and soapstone . . . " (*Statistics,* 726; cf. *Improvement,* 161), and it had most of the design elements of his Union J (except that it had end pavilions and a modified fenestration; for an illustration, see *A History of Spartanburg County* [n.p., 1940: WPA American Guide Series], opp. 209; Fig. 36A herein).

Sumter

The Jay CH is discussed in the text. For the appropriations, cf. *Acts,* 1817, 100 and 1818, 98; for a contract date of 5 March 1820 and for expenditures, *Improvement,* 159. The specifications are nearly identical to those for Colleton (the Beaufort drawings of 1819 were to have been used [*Improvement,* 2], but Thomas Baker had made a change [letter of John B. Miller to Robert Mills, 16 Aug. 1821; SCDAH 302-2]). Plans and specifications which are dated 1 July 1839 and which were prepared for the renovation of this building reveal that it was built with a hipped roof and courtroom on the ground floor (Figs. 10-11). By 1840 it was to have its second floor lowered, its courtroom moved upstairs, and a pedimented portico added. These changes are reflected in a photograph (Fig. 10B) of the building that shows a closed-in side window on the second story at a higher level than the others; the portico had subsequently had a parapet added (Anne King Gregorie, *History of Sumter County* [Sumter, 1954], 289). Mills described the CH and J as "handsome" (*Statistics,* 742), an adjective usually reserved for his own buildings, but he was not involved in the design of the CH, and the historical marker stating that he designed it is incorrect. The J was authorized in 1826 and additional funds were approved in 1827 (4 *Stat.* 301, 351), but the need for a new building had been mentioned in an 1820 report prepared while Jay was still on the BPW (*Improvement,* 33). The surviving elevation resembles the Pendleton J and the Beaufort CH and is similar to Jay's courthouse and jail designs, but is probably not by him. Although Thomas Baker left the BPW in 1820, he was a commissioner for Sumter, which explains his signature on the drawings. The signature is in a different hand from the specifications and appear to be for the purposes of identifying the drawing as part of a contractual agreement. E.R. McIver, the former SPB and one of the contractors for the Sumter J, also had access to the Jay drawing and presumably he or McIver prepared the Sumter J plans. The agreement is dated 24 Jan. 1828 with a stipulation that the work be completed by 1 Oct. 1830 (SCDAH).

Union

A CH was approved in 1823 and is unquestionably by Mills because he was then SPB (*Acts,* 118). It and the jail were to be of brick, but the quality of local brick forced Mills to face them with stone (Report of Robert Mills to the President of the BPW, 30 Nov. 1822;

SCDAH 1822-112-7/8; cf. 10-3-ND-598 and 10-4-1822-112; letters of Robert G. Mills [of Chesterville] to Robert Mills, 8 Sept. 1822, and of Joseph Winn to Robert Mills, 25 Aug. 1822). The CH followed the Marlborough prototype (for illustrations, Union County Historical Foundation, *A History of Union County, South Carolina* [Greenville, 1977], 15-16. These photographs are of the building being dismantled in c. 1912 and show the addition that had been made "to conform precisely with the outward appearance of said building" [a specification in the contract with William Herbeson dated 29 Jan., 1857; SCDAH. Cf. 12 *Stat.* 420]). The J was built during 1822-1823 (with an 1824 appropriation to cover extra costs; SCDAH mfm. 7-7C93). Mills described his buildings at Union as "a handsome stone courthouse and jail, upon the most improved plan . . . " (*Statistics*, 757).

Williamsburg (Kingstree)

A new CH was ordered by a resolution of 1821 and the major portion of the appropriation was authorized in 1822 (*Acts*, 102). Frederick Wesner, an amateur architect and a subcontractor for the Fireproof Building, had completed the work by 1825 (*Acts*, 16. Ravenel, *Architects*, 137-146). Funds to enlarge and renovate the surviving building by adding rooms at the back were made in Dec. 1853 and Dec. 1854 to the design of "P.H. Hammarskold" (SCDAH, Petition, 10 December 1855; he complained that no funds had been left for "any pay to the Architect, which is customary at 5% percent on the expenditure . . . ." Cf. Ravenel, *Architects*, 241-243). In 1883, a fire gutted the second story, but records stored on the first story were protected from damage by the brick vaulting (William Willis Boddie, *History of Williamsburg* . . . [Columbia, 1923], 462); the roof was rebuilt, and the cornice was probably Victorianized at this time (illustrated in Carl Julien and James McBride Dabbs, *Pee Dee Panorama* [Columbia, 1951], 54; Fig. 22 herein).

A new J was authorized in 1823 (*Acts*, 118), the year Mills was SPB. It was destroyed after a new J was authorized in 1858 (12 *Stat.* 587; built to the designs of the Charleston architect, Edward C. Jones).

York (Yorkville)

The CH was authorized in 1821 and built between 1822 and 1824 (*Acts,* 1822, 102; SCDAH mfm 7-7C93, 7-8A50). Its exterior followed the Marlborough plan but its interior was "amphitheatrical in its form, with a segment spherical ceiling" (*Statistics*, 772). It was enlarged with an appropriation of 1851 (12 *Stat.* 73; SCDAH, Petition, 18 November 1851). A photograph of a wood engraving of this courthouse is in the SCL and is captioned: "THE ORIGINAL COURT HOUSE. The above is probably the only accurate picture of the original York county court house that has ever been made. It was secured for an illustrated write-up of the town of Yorkville in 1889, and was the result of much labor and expense. Because of difficulties well understood by photographers, it was impractical to get a photograph that would take in the entire building, and it was necessary to take several pictures to enable the engravers to produce what was wanted. The above picture is a faithful reproduction of the building, except the walls, which appear to be stucco, showed natural brick. The original engraving of the above was burned with The Enquirer office in 1890, and this picture is a photographic reproduction of the cut as it was printed in 1889."

A new J was authorized in 1825 (*Acts*, 17) and built in 1827-1828 (SCDAH mfm 7-8A50, SCDAH contract dated 22 May 1827). The surviving building does not resemble the work of Mills. Although a 21 February 1822 advertisement in the *Charleston Courier* (cited by Ravenel, *Architects*, 110) calls for bids for "York — Building Court House and Jail" (see Appendix II), the appropriation of 1821 included only $2,000 to repair the existing jail (Committe on Public Buildings, report on the report of the Board of Public Works; SCDAH 1821-99-01. See *Improvement*, 120, 157.).

APPENDIX II

SELECTED DOCUMENTS

(1)   Specifications for the Colleton Courthouse and Jail, 18 May 1820. Attributed to William Jay (SCDAH, Public Improvement, 1800-1830, Buildings).

Specifications of the Materials and Workmanship to be employed in building the Court House to be erected in Colleton District at Walterborough.

Bricklayers Work.

The building to be of Brick, Fifty by forty feet from out to out. The Foundation to be sunk a proper depth but not less than 2½ feet and laid on piling if necessary, and to be raised 2½ ft. above the surface of the ground. The wall to be of the thickness of 3 bricks or 29 In. The first story to be 18 feet in the clear, in which there are 10 windows & 3 doors, the wall to be 2½ bricks or 2 ft. thick to the level of the joists. The second story to be 12 feet in the clear, to have 13 windows, the wall to be 2 bricks or 19 In. thick. The cornice at the eave to be of brick, a brick & a half or a 14 In. wall to extend the length of the building, to be sunk a sufficient depth & raised 2½ ft. above the ground on which the partition dividing the Ct. room from the stairs is to rest. All of which brick work to be done with bricks of the best kind, & laid in good strong mortar having at least 1½ barrel of unslacked stone lime or 25 bushels of shell lime to the thousand bricks. The walls to be well secured with 4 ties of bond timber placed in the centre of the wall. Wooden blocks or scantling to be worked in the wall to which the furring is to be nailed, the wall plates to be well bedded. The roof to be coverd with glazed pan tile pointed both within & without. The lobby to be paved with bricks or Tiles bedded in strong mortar, all the windows and Doors to be recessed 4½ In. & to shew not more than 1½ In. of the frame to the weather. The exterior of the building to be finished in all respects as represented by the plan.

Plasterers Work.

The sides of the Court room from the height of the surbase to the ceiling & the ceiling as also the ceilings of the lobby passages and offices to be lathed & plastered with 3 Coats of Mortar. The cornice of the Ct. room to be done in stucco agreeably to the plan which is drawn to full size. The outside of the building is to be roughcast & ornamented having rustics agreeably to the plan and coloured with roman cement.

Stone Masons Work.

The outer steps as also the sills of the Doors & windows to be of wrought stone.

Carpenters Work.

Thee ties of bond timber 6 by 6 In. one tie 6 by 4½ to be well framed & spliced. The joists of the first & second story to be 13 by 3 In. let down 1 In. on the plates & a sufficient number dove tailed to the plates all of which joists to be placed at the distance of 16 In. from centre to centre, sprung & bridged if necessary. The floors to be laid with narrow boards free from sap, planed, tongued, grooved, and nailed from the top. The principal rafters to be 10 In. at bottom, 8 at top, & 5 In. thick. Tye beams 12 in. by 5. King posts 13 by 5 in. Hipped rafters 10 in. at bottom 8 at top & 3 In. thick. Purloins 7 by 4 In. Centre rafters 6 in. at bottom 5 at top & 3 In. thick. Cuppled rafters in proportion. Ceiling joists 5 in. by 2, all of which joists & rafters to be placed at the distance of 16 in. from centre to centre. Laths for tiling 2½ in. wide by 1 in thick. The partition which divides the stairs from Ct. room to be of Studs 8 In. Square & placed at the distance of 22 In. from centre to centre. All the other partitions to be of 2 In. plank & trussed, the plank to be planed on both sides, tongued, grooved and beaded. The sides of the Court room as high as the surbase, the back of the jury boxes as high as the upper seat and the sides of the lobby, passages & offices to be lined with boards planed, tongued, grooved & beaded. All of which boards both for the partitions & lining to be put up vertically. The Ct. room to have a neat base & surbase moulding. All the other rooms, passages & c. a plain base & surbase. The window frames in the Ct. room to be boxed. The sash to be double hung with best cordage & brass pullies & to have sash lifters & sash fastenings. The windows in the Ct. room to be set high enough to admit the seats to be on a level with the floor of the Judges bench, which is to be 3½ ft. above the floor of the Ct. room & the floor of the criminals box on a level with it. All the other windows to be placed at the usual height. All the windows to have shutters & to be hung on the outside, to be 2 In. thick, bound & moulded on one side. The outer doors to be framed bead & Flush out side & moulded within to be 2½ In. thick. The front Door to be a double door 4½ wide. The centre door entering Ct. room, to be a double door 6 ft. wide & double wrought to have an eliptical fan light above, sashed & glazed. All other doors 7½ ft. high 3½ wide, 2 In. thick framed & moulded on both sides. All the windows & doors to have plain jam casings, soffits & single faced architraves except those in the Ct. room which are to have panneled casings & soffits & double faced architraves or pilasters, two elipticall, Arches as shewn by the plan & neatly finished. All the sash to be ovolo-double Flanked. The sash of the lower Story to have 32 lights, those of the upper 24 lights. The size of the glass 12 by 14 In. The judges & clerks desks to be panneled & capped with a neat rail & bannisters as [also the jury & criminals boxes] to be capped with bannisters & rail. The steps & Spectators seats to be [finished agreeably to] the plan. The stairs to have turned newels [sqr. bannesters, a worked hand & half hand rail. Steps one & a half In. thick. Returned nosing.] Risers mitered to the string under the stairs ceiled with boards or plastered. The furring not to exceed 18 In. from centre to centre.

Blacksmiths Work.

The roof to be well strapped with Iron. The doors & windows to be hung with good & substantial hinges and to have the requisite bolts & Fastenings both within & without. The doors of the lower story to have 10 In. Locks with brass knobs & the doors of the upper story to have 8 In. locks with brass knobs. The outer doors to have two Keys to each lock. Nails, brads, screws & c.

Painters & Glaziers Work.

All the sash to be primed & glazed. The Doors of the lower story, the judges & Clerks desk to be painted a Mahogany colour. The doors above, wash boards & rails to be painted a chocolate colour. All the rest of the wood work to have two coats of paint of a good standing colour.

Specification of the Materials & Workmanship to be employed in building the Jail to be erected at Walterborough Colleton District.

The building to be of Brick 45 feet by 35 feet from out to out, to be covered with glazed pan Tile, pointed with strong mortar within & without. The Foundation sunk a sufficient depth but not less than 2½ feet & raised 2½ feet above ground, to be 4 bricks or 3 ft. 4 In. thick & from thence to the full height of the building 3 bricks or two ft. 5 In. thick. The first story to be 14 ft. and the second story 11 feet in the clear. The bricks to be laid in strong mortar having 25 bushels of shell lime or one & a half barls. of stone lime to the thousand brick. The walls to be well secured with bond timber. The Doors & windows to have stone sills. The back & Front steps to be of Stone. The first floor of Joists to be 13 In. by 3 placed 18 In. from centre to centre to be supported by a 14 In. wall running thro the centre of the building. This floor to be laid with 1¼ In. boards not exceeding 9 In. wide free from Sap, to be planed, tongued & grooved. The lower rooms to be divided as shewn by the plan, to be of studs 8 In. Square an[d] placed 22 In. from centre to centre. The sides & ceilings as als[o] the passage & ceiling to be lined with Inch boards, planed tongued & grooved. Jamb casings, soffits & seats to be plane with a bead on the edge, the partition Doors to be batten & made with board not exceeding 5 In. in width. The two out side doors to be batten & cross lined. The front to be double & 2½ thick, the stairs to be plain, with newels, rail & bannesters. The steps to be 1¼ In. thick. Shutters of this story to be hung on the outside, to be batten & double, planed, tongued grooved & beaded. The windows to be sashed & glazed, doors & windows to be of the size represented by the plan.

Second story, the upper & lower joists to be 10 In. by 4 In., the studs of the partitions 8 In. Sqr. All of which joists & studs to be placed at the distance of 6 In., 3 by 5 In. scantling to be worked in the wall not more than 6 In. apart, to extend from the floor to the ceiling. The floors, sides ceilings & windows of all the rooms & the sides of the partition in the passages to be lined with 2½ In. plank, planed, tongued, grooved & well spiked. The windows to be double grated and made perfectly secure. A bar of Iron to be well spiked across the heads of the plank that line the walls below the windows & to extend at least 18 In. on each side of the windows. The entrance into the rooms to have two doors. Those opening in rooms to be Iron grated the squares to be not more than 8 In. Those opening into the passage to [be] of plank, to be 3 In. thick cross lined & well spiked. These doors to be hung with substantial hinges 3 pr. to each door the centre staple reversed, & to have the requisite bolts & bars and locks of the best quality as also to the outer doors. The windows to have inside shutters with proper fastenings. The roof to be framed with principal rafters of the best timber & of sufficient strenght & well strapped with Iron, the rafters to be not more than 18 In. from centre to centre. All the doors & windows to be recessed. The shutters to be hung with substantial hinges & to have the necessary fastenings within & without. The building to be roughcast & coloured with roman cement. All the wood work to have two coats of paint of a good colour.

And be it further understood that in finishing the work whether of Bricklayers, Carpenters, Blacksmiths or Painters & Glaziers it must be done in the best manner possible, furnishing all and every material necessary for the completion of said work of the best quality without omitting any thing here specified or embraced in the annexed plans tho not here distinctly expressed or any thing necessary to the completion of said Buildings. I agree to complete the said Buildings agreeably to the plans and the specifications for the sum of Twenty Thousand Seven hundred and fifty Dollars on or before the first of January 1822.

18 May 1820   Wm. N. Thompson

[N.B.   The words supplied within brackets are from the nearly identical specifications for the Sumter Courthouse.]

(2)   **Advertisement for bids by Robert Mills, 21 February 1822, in** *The Charleston Courier.*

Public Buildings. The subscriber, acting Commissioner of the Board of Public Works, being now in this City, will receive proposals until the 1st of March, for supplying the materials of Brick, Lime, Lumber, Iron and Stone, as also the different kinds of Mechanical work, required in the execution of the Court House and Jails named below.

The Proposals to state the terms, when the several articles can be delivered, and the price of the same; the materials must be of the best quality. The description and nature of the various kinds of work to be done, can be had by applying as above.

Williamsburg — Building Court House.

Newberry — Building Court House.

Union — Building Jail.

Spartanburg — Building Jail.

Lancaster — Building Jail.

York — Building Court House and Jail.

Greenville — Building Court House.

Robert Mills, 169 [?] Bay.
February 21.

(3) **Report of the Legislative Committee on Buildings, 16 December 1823 (SCDAH, 10-4-1823-207).**

The joint committee of both Houses on Public Buildings to whom was referred the Report of the Superintendent of Public Buildings Respectfully report. —

That they have with much attention examined the same, together with the Superintendent personally & are of opinion that it will be necessary to build during the Year Eighteen Hundred & Twenty four, Three new Court Houses and Two new Gaols; Therefore recommend that the following sums be appropriated for the same, to wit; for Darlington Court House, Ten Thousand Dollars — Union Court House, Ten Thousand Dollars; Horry Court House, Ten Thousand Dollars; Williamsburg Gaol, Eight Thousand Dollars; Marion Gaol Eight Thousand Dollars; They further find that other Public Buildings require repairs, and therefore recommend the following appropriations be made to put them in complete repair, (To wit) Horry Gaol, Three thousand Dollars; Orangeburg Gaol, Three Thousand Five Hundred Dollars; Newbury Court House, Six hundred & thirty two Dollars — College buildings, Two Thousand Dollars; State House — Three hundred Dollars; Arsenel in Charleston, Two Hundred and fifty Dollars; Barnwell Court House & Gaol, Eight hundred Dollars; Greenville Gaol, One hundred Dollars; Pendleton Court House Two Hundred & one Dollars nine & a half cents; Laurance [Laurens] Court House & Gaol, Six hundred Dollars; — Abbeville Court House, Fifty Dollars; Chester Court House, Two hundred & fifty Dollars; Edgefield Court House, Two hundred Dollars; Sumpter Court House, Two hundred Dollars; Fairfield Court House & Gaol, Three hundred & fifty Dollars; if so much of the respective sums be necessary; — Your Committee have further been informed by the Superintendent of Public Buildings that it will be necessary to appropriate additional sums to complete some of the buildings now under contract, they therefore beg leave to recommend the following additional sums to be appropriated, To wit, For York Court House Five hundred & Twenty One Dollars; Union Gaol. Four Thousand, Four hundred & thirty four Dollars & fourteen Cents; Lancaster Gaol, Two Thousand Dollars; Your Committee will observe here, that the Contractors for the two last named buildings, received considerable sums in advance & afterwards one refused to comply with his contract and the other absconded, their Bonds however your Committee has been informed are placed in the hands of the Solicitor for collection — Spartanburg, Nine Hundred & fifteen Dollars; Charleston Gaol, Five thousand Dollars; Lexington Court House, Seventy five Dollars; Your Committee further report that they have been informed that encroachments have been made on the Court House Lot in Richland District; they therefore submit the propriety of making an enquiry into the same —

G.W. Morrall
Chairman

[on the reverse:]

Report of the joint Committee of both Houses on Public Buildings on the Report of the Superintendent of Public Buildings.

In Senate 16th Decr. 1823. Resolved that this House do agree to the report. Ordered that it be sent to the House of Representatives for concurrence. By order of Senate, *Wm. D. Martin,* C.S.

Agreed to.
To be returned.
H.R. To Senate.

In the House of Representatives, December 18th, 1823. Resolved that the House do concur with the Senate in the foregoing Report Ordered that it be returned. By order of the House R. Anderson C.H.R.

(4) **Specifications for the Horry Courthouse, attributed to Robert Mills. Horry "Commissioners Book — Public Buildings" (1802-1851), 20 May 1824. Accompanying the bond of Russell Warren, p. 6-9. SCDAH typescript; W.P.A. Project 65-33-118.**

Specifications of Court House Horry District, Conwayborough The drawings Shewing the dimensions Elevation windows Doors & c & c being a part of the Contract will wholly and entirely govern the Execution of the Building, Using the materials detailed below, viz: the extreme walls of Brick, the inside of Brick to the Court Room floor to be laid in good mortar of Lime and Sharp Sand the Arches covering the Office's to be groin. The passage Barrel arch arcade groin arches all grouted the wall to be timbered and Lathed to receive the plastering throughout, arcade passages to be paved with Brick tile, Piers and Portico Brick the Columns Brick and Stuccoe, all the inside wall and ceilings to be plastered, Stone Sills to all the doors & windows Steps to Portico and facing bound, flagstone to Portico and pavement in front. three Sides of the Building to be paved with brick. Woodwork to consist of ribs and Sheathing for centres of the Arches Doors to offices, bead & butt six pannel with Jamb casing 3-6 by 7 ft 1½ in thick, Skirting or wash board to Offices 8 in high, Windows as per drawing 16 lights 10 by 12 Glass, 1¼ in Sash Single hung with Jamb complete. Shutters inside folding, 2 Six pannel doors per drawing. front & Back 1½ each in 2 leaves with Solid 6 in rabbit & bead frames. Jamb Casing & moulding with a lock on the front door, 2 fancy transome, over the above door, 4 plan chimney mantle pieces to Offices. The Contractor shall have liberty to alter Portico and Steps as he pleases for the improvement of the front of the Same all the Stone work Shall be of the best quality of Free stone, Principal Story 6 windows with circular heads 24 square lights pr drawing 1½ in Sash Single hung. 2 do with Side lights as above centre Sash double hung, 1 circular transom window over Judges Seat pr drawing 1 front door with side lights and Court room door each in 2 leaves 1½ In thick finished as per drawing. 2 Six pannel doors to Jury rooms 1½ in thick with casing and moulding complete 36 rises to s[t]airs 3 feet wide strong newels & hand rails square balluatrade thick Stuff for S[t]eps 10 rises to Judges Seat window platform to ditto, front pannel circular & ballustrade to ditto Clerks desk with low ballustrading to ditto in front. With drawers & pigon holes to ditto, Lawyers table in Sections rising from the Clerk's desk, Spectators and Jury Seats with backs. Flooring to gallery 1¼ inch plank tongued and grooved on 3 by 9 Joice — raking down the gallery 3 ft with Suitable railing for the Seats at Suitable distance, ballustrading in Front from 2 to 3 foot high, ditto round the well of the stairs. Skirting 8 in high rooms Steed ["sic"] partition to jury rooms, Roof frame principal rafters, collar beams and perloins & jack rafters with shingle covering. 1 girder under the front of the gallery. eave cornice according to drawing framing roof & ceiling portico. All the wood work to be painted colors directed by the Commissioners — Shelves in Office Table & Benches in Jury rooms and locks to all the Doors. Iron railing to Steps.

(5) **Edgefield Jail agreement, 15 April 1825. (SCDAH, Bonds)**

South Carolina
Edgefield District

This agreement entered into the fifteenth day of April in the year of our Lord one thousand, eight hundred & twenty five between Benjamin Frazier, Allen B. Addison, William Blackburn, Abner Blocker & Whitfield Brooks Commissioners of Public buildings for Edgefield District on the one part and Campbell Humphries of the District of Union of the other part to the purport and effect following, that whereas the Legislature of this State did make at the last session an appropriation of eight thousand dollars for the purpose of building a jail at Edgefield Courthouse, and the said Commissioners having entered into a contract with the said Campbell Humphries to erect said building, they do hereby covenant to & with the said C. Humphries to allow him the sum of eight thousand dollars for the erection & completion of said jail; to be paid by orders on the Treasurer of the upper division of the State for such sums & at such times during the progress of the work, as the Commissioners may deem reasonable & just, with & under the express understanding & agreement that whenever the aforesaid Commissioners or a majority of them shall draw an order for money on the Treasurer, the work that may then be done and all materials for building either of rock, wood or brick prepared by the said C. Humphries or his workman are immediately to become the property of the Commissioners, and all title, property, claim or controll in or over the Same to vest in the said Commissioners, provided the said Campbell Humphries after drawing the money, shall either die, or neglect or refuse to go on with the work of the said jail. And the said Campbell Humphries on his part doth covenant to and with the said Benjamin Frazier, Allen B. Addison, William Blackburn Abner Blocker & Whitfield Brooks Commissioners, as aforesaid to erect & complete a jail at the place designated by the Commissioners of the dimensions & after the manner following. The house to be forty eight feet in length and thirty seven feet in breadth, to be built of rock (except the partition walls not connected with the criminal rooms which are to be of brick, laid in lime mortar in the proportions of one bushel of roack [rock] lime to four of sharp sand — The out side wall to be twenty four inches thick and the inner walls of the criminal rooms to be eighteen inches thick & the others fourteen inches thick — The elevation of the basement story to be ten feet from floor to floor, with an open arcade in front supported by two pillars of rock, neatly hewed & arched — This story to be divided into six rooms & a passage for a flight of stairs, to be of rock. Three rooms on one side, one in the centre & two on the other side with the stair way, with substantial & neatly made door shutters & thirteen glass windows of fifteen lights each. The second story to be ten feet in elevation & divided into seven rooms. Three of these intended for criminals & convicts are to be built in the following manner, the rock on the out side course of the walls to be dowelled together at each joint. The inside walls to be ceiled with two inch oak plank spiked to the walls by three courses of iron spikes driven into solid pieces of timber let into the wall at proper intervals. The floor and ceiling over head to be of two inch heart pine plank. The ceiling on the walls to extend two inches above the ceiling head and two inches below the floor. The joists to be ten inches, in dimensions, & placed not more than three inches apart, to consist of two tiers, crossing each other at right angles. To each of these rooms there are to be two door shutters, one on the inside to be of bar iron & the other of oak plank, to be four inches thick & well spiked each shutter to hang on three pair of hinges on both the inner & out side of the rooms. Locks to each door of the most approved & substantial kind, one of which to be made after the model of those on the Union jail. The shutters to the remaining rooms in this story to be of good oak plank, four inches thick well spiked, & to have good hinges & locks. The apartments intended for negroes to be ceiled as discribed in the rooms for criminals & the others neatly plastered. The windows in this story to be horizontal, except the three in front, which are to be arched, with iron grates. The sills & caps of the horizontal windows and of the doors for the three criminal rooms to be of solid hewed rock, to extend the whole width of the wall with a rabbit of three inches cut on the outside of the jams to receive the out side shutters. The floor of this story to be laid of two inch plank & the roof to be of heart shingles of the best pine, painted or tared. The walls of the house where not ceiled to be plastered in a neat & durable manner. The wood work of the house to be neatly painted. There are to be four chimneys & fire places. The whole to be completed in a neat, substantial and workmanlike manner equal in execution in every particular & after the model of the

47

Union jail & possession given to the Commissioners on or before the first day of March next. And the said C. Humphries doth further covenant & agree with the said Commissioners that whenever they shall draw an order for money in his favor on the Treausrer of the State that he the said C. Humphries upon the receipt of the money will permit the said Commissioners to take possession of the building and all the materials before specified the right title & property in the same to vest in the said Commissioners to be held by them for the benefit of the state and as a guaranty for their own safety, provided as before that the said C. Humphries after receiving the money shall die or fail or refuse to presecute the work either in person or by his representative in case of his death. And the said Campbell Humphries doth further agree to depend for payment on the State and no further to hold the Commissioners responsible, than an honest and conscientious discharge of the trust, resposed in them by the Legislature.

In witness wherof the parties have hereunto set their hands and seals the day & year first above written.

Signed and executed in presence of H. Mims.

Whit. Brooks	(Seal)
A.B. Addison	(Seal)
Benj. Frazier	(Seal)
[blank]	(Seal)
[blank]	(Seal)
C. Humphrys	(Seal)

(6)   **Chesterfield Courthouse documents, 1825-1827. (SCDAH, Bonds).**

(A)   **Specifications by Robert Mills, 7 March 1825.**

Specifications

The Building for the Court House in Chesterfield District is to be built of Stone and Brick, in the Village of Chesterfield, on the public Lot directly at the west end of the old Court House and fronting the Jail — size Fifty by forty feet, form and dimentions given in the drafts, a good foundation of stone to be raised twelve inches above the surface of the earth, Turn groin arches over the four Offices grouted, one fireplace to each room; arcade over the passage passing between passage and offices paved with good smoothe tile grouted; and walls to be plastered hard finish; stone sills and caps to office doors and windows well dressed; Stone Steps to Portico resting on Brick arches, iron hand rails and Balisters to each. Brick Collums rough cast and painted marble colour; with neat stone base and capping. Foundation secured by water Table course of brick projecting two inches, over the external wall. All the walls are to be laid in good strong lime mortar solid through. The first story to commence two feet thick, and to be secured by interties of iron of the following description (To Wit) six bars, one and one fourth inch Square, to extend across the building under the court room floor, headed at each end with axe bar iron eighteen inches in length five do. crossing length ways in the same manner, all of which are to be concealed within the work. The partition walls and walls to second story eighteen inches thick, walls to third story fourteen inches thick. The whole of the outer walls to be neatly finished; and plastered hard finish on the inside — wooden cornish under the eaves of the principal, finished in handsome stile. Courtroom and portico to be paved with best quality of tile and grouted, portico to be finished in handsome stile with wooden cornish. Stone sills for court room door and fourteen windows eighteen lights each 10 by 12 Glass, with neat stone arching over each well dressed; sashes and frames with three coats of paint. — One pannelled door hung in halves three Butts to each half, fancy transom lights over, with one superior Knob Lock — Four office doors two inches thick, six pannel bead and butt, jamcasings three feet six inches by seven feet, one rim'd Lock to each — sixteen windows to the offices 12 lights each 10 by 12

Glass window shutters 1¼ inch thick, pannel'd hung on the inside in halves, with good iron fastenings. — Wash boards & Chair boards to offices, court and Jury rooms with moulded caps; seats for Jurors, Spectators and cliants, permanent with backs and raised to suit the commissioners. — Nine Tables for Attorneys two feet & half by four feet made in circular form, eighteen windsor chairs for the same, strong and neat. — One prisoners box. — Judges seat and Clerks Desk to correspond with each other, finished neatly and painted as the commissioners may direct. Two flights of stairs up to Jury rooms, with cylinder hand rails, round nuels and balisters; one girder 8 inches by 12 inches across length ways and supported by two turned wooden collums and two semi do 12 inches at Base and 8 inches at top rising directly over the partition walls, ceiling over head tongued and groved, painted white with neat plane wooden cornish, Joist 3 by 12 inches over the courtroom. Stair case, washboards, all the furniture and every other part which may require painting will be done as the commissioners may require. Jury rooms to be floored with 1¼ inch quartered plank, and divided by wooden partitions, cieled overhead & painted white one good pannelled door to each room, with one Knob Lock & hung with large Butts. Thirteen windows 15 lights each 10 by 12 glass with stone sills and arched over with brick. Four Tables 3 feet wide and 10 feet long with two benches to each, for the Jury rooms. Four tables 3 feet wide 5 feet long with pidgeon holes and shelves sufficient to hold all the Books and papers, for the Offices. Roofing framed with collar beams 3 by 5 and rafters 5 by 7 with principle rafters, braces, purloins and Jacks, one trap door with step ladder. Sheating gauged to equal thickness, shingled with best pine shingles guaged to 3/4 inch at butt, and drawn true to average 4 inches in width, when jointed, length twenty one inches, the roof to be painted slate colour. The outside walls are to be painted brick colour and neatly penciled with white lead. The materials are to be of the best that the country will afford, subject to the inspection of the commissioners, or a majority of them. And the Building is to be completed in eighteen months from the date of the contract, and done in every respect in a workmanlike manner. Also the sum of Twenty five dollars to be paid to Robert Mills for the drafts furnished the commissioners — and the sum of Five dollars to be paid Mason R. Lyon for advertising in his paper for proposals for the said Building.

We the commissioners of Public Buildings for the district aforesaid having adopted the plan furnished by Robert Mills, with a few alterations, do agree to the foregoing specifications.

Chesterfield Court House March 7th 1825	W. Ellerby Peter May Wm. McBride John Evans Peter L. Robeson	Commissioners

(B)   Bond, 10 May 1825.

The State of South Carolina
Chesterfield District

Know all men by these presents that we John Chapman, John Craig and Archibald McDonald are holden and firmly bound unto Thomas Harrison Treasurer of the upper division, in the full and just sum of Seventeen Thousand and forty dollars good and lawful money of the said State, to be paid unto the said Thomas Harrison, or to his successors treasurers of the said upper division, to which payment well and truly to be made and done we bind ourselves, our Heirs, Executors, and administrators, for the whole and in the whole, severally and separately, firmly by these presents. Seal'd with our seals and dated this tenth day of May in the year of our Lord one thousand eight hundred and twenty five.

The condition of the above obligation is such, that if the above bound John Chapman, shall furnish materials and Build or cause to be built a new Court House in the Village of

Chesterfield and district aforesaid at the west end of the old Court House, of such form and dimentions and of such materials as are discribed in the specifications hereunto attached, within eighteen months from the date hereon, and shall fulfil in every respect all and every the items contained in the said specifications to the satisfaction of the commissioners of Public Buildings [or to the satisfaction of (?)] a majority of them, then this obligation to be void and of none effect or else to remain in full force and virtue.

Signed and seal'd in the presence of
D.A. Campbell   John Chapman   (seal)
Wm. Middleton   John Craig   (seal)
                                                    A. Mc. Donald   (seal)

We the undersigned commissioners of Public Buildings for Chesterfield district have let the Building of the new Court House to the above named John Chapman for the sum of Eight thousand five hundred and twenty dollars, and approve of his Bond & security.

Chesterfield Court House   W. Ellerbe
May 10th. 1825   Peter May
                                                         Wm McBride
                                                         John Evans
                                                         Peter L. Robeson

(C) Alterations, 1827

The State of South Carolina

To John Chapman Jr. for extra work done on the New Court House in Chesterfield District by order of the Commissioners of Public Buildings

	Dr.
To 38330 Brick Lime & Laying inclusive @ 16.00 pr. M	$ 609.28
N.B. This charge is for raising the walls of the first & third stories (including the Portico) each two feet higher than is specified in the former contract.	
To Plaistering including the materials for the above extra walls	88.00
To Six extra stone steps for Portico at $15.50 each	93.00
To 100 feet Raking Cornice (omitted in former contract) at 50¢	50.00
To 33 pair Window Blinds @ $4	132.00
To altering Window Shutters	3.50
To 70 ft. Railing & Balusters for Court room @ 75¢	52.50
" 2 Large Folding doors for Passage @ $12. each	24.00
" 1 Knob Lock for Do. 2.25, 4 Bolts for Do. 2.00	4.25
" Materials for making & Hanging the same	5.00
" Painting Do. $3.00, 2 extra pair Butt Hinges for office doors 75¢	3.75
" 28 Back fastenings for office windows @ 15¢	4.20
" 4 Extra Windows & stone sills	44.20
" Materials for making & painting Do.	8.00
" Setting the 4 Sills @ 50¢	2.00
" 24 Extra Joists 4 by 10 — 43 ft long — 1208 ft @ 2½	30.20
" 66 pr. Hinges for Blinds @ 50¢	33.00

" 50 Doz. Screws for putting on Do.	6.25
" 31 inside window fastenings @ 12½	3.87½
" 62 outside Do. Do. @ 15	9.30
	1206.30½
Amot. Brot. forward	1206.30½
To Paints & painting Blinds	$ 165.00
" plank & other materials furnished & not enumerated	122.75
" putting gutters round the portico	8.00
" extra materials for Judges seat	5.00
	$1507.05½
deduct for difference in quantity of Iron not put into the building as contracted for	27.05½
	$1480.00

This is to certify that we the undersigned commissioners of public buildings for Chesterfield District have this day met for the purpose of examing & receiving the new Court House contracted to be built by John Chapman Jr. & have found the building in every respect to be equal to the contract & specifications — We further certify the foregoing to be a supplemental contract made with said John Chapman for certain extra work omitted in the previous contract, & necessary to complete said building.

Chesterfield Ct. Ho. Oct. 29th 1827	Commissioners of Pulic Buildings
	Peter L. Robeson
	Wm McBride
	Peter May
	John Evans

(7)   Kershaw Courthouse agreement, 12 May 1825 (SCDAH, Bonds).

Articles of Agreement

Made this twelfth day of May in the year of Our Lord one thousand eight hundred and twenty five between the Commissioners of Public building of Kershaw District South Carolina on the one part and William Robinson Carpenter and Contractor of the Town of Camden in above said District on the other part.

Witnesseth

That whereas the said commissioners intend to erect a certain Building or Court House in the Town of Camden on the public square and to employ in the erection of the said Court house and in its decoration a quantity of work and materials in Brick, wood, Stone, Stucco, Iron & c. And whereas he the said William Robinson is willing and does hereby undertake and contract to provide all the Materials and labor of every description required to complete the said building of the best quality and done in the most workmanlike manner agreeably to the designs of Robert Mills Architect under the direction of the said Commissioners and according to the schedule and description hereunto annexed and which form part of this agreement,

Now therefore it is agreed between the parties hereunto in form and manner following — And first on the part of the said Commissioners.

1st.   That in consideration and in part payment of the work and materials hereby stipulated to be finished and on the conditions herein after specified they the said commissioners will pay or cause to be paid unto the said William Robinson the sum of three thousand dollars in advance at the signing of these articles and he giving of good bond and security.

    2nd.   That soon as the Building is half finished on which the Commissioners shall be the Judges they will pay or cause to be paid the further sum of three thousand dollars.

    3rd.   That as soon as the building is completed or this agreement fully complied with the sum of two thousand seven hundred and ninety eight dollars in all the sum of Eight thousand seven hundred and ninety eight dollars, payments to be made by drafts on the Treasurer of the State for the upper Division.

    4th.   And on the part of the said William Robinson it is hereby agreed as follows to wit. That on considereation of the said sums to be to him duly paid at the periods above recited amounting in all to Eight thousand and seven hundred and ninety eight dollars he shall and will at his proper cost and expence provide all the materials and work required in the erection and completion of the said Court house agreeably to the annexed schedule and according to the designs of the said Robert Mills hereunto annexed and which form part of this agreement the materials of the best quality and the work done in the most workmanlike manner making every exertion to have the building completely finished in all the month of May One thousand eight hundred and twenty seven (1827) under the penalty of five thousand dollars unavoidable accidents or bad seasons excepted.

    5th.   Should any other work be ordered in *writing* to be done by the commissioners more than is stated in the specifications annexed or should any alterations be made by them the same shall be valued according to its worth such change shall in no wise however invalidate this contract.

    In witness wherof the Parties hereunto set their hands and Seals this twelfth day of May in the year of Our Lord one thousand eight hundred and twenty five.

Witnessed by Joshua Reynolds

Commissioners

Wm Robinson
Tho. Salmond
Lewis Ciples
W.W. Lang
Alexander Young

1 Savannah houses attributed to William Jay: (A) Richard Richardson House, 1818; (B) William Scarbrough House, 1819 (restoration drawing).

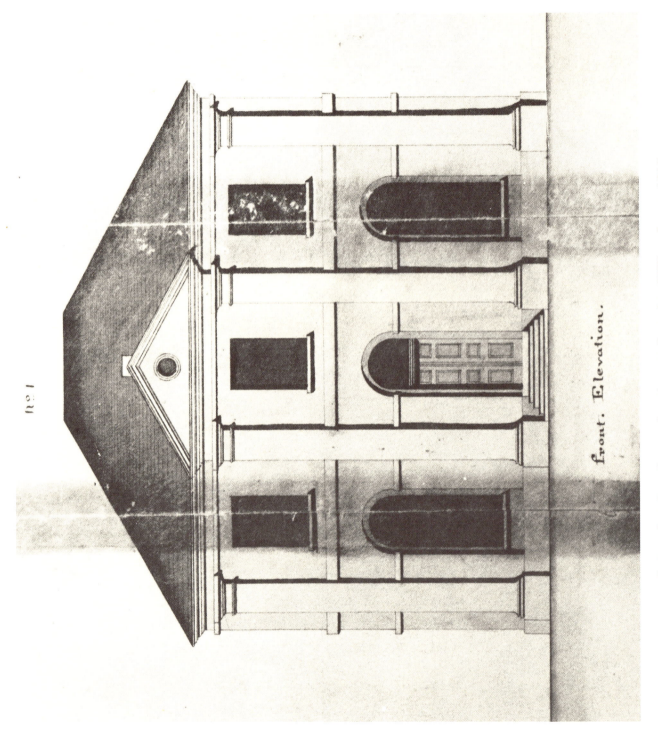

2 Beaufort Courthouse elevation attributed to William Jay, c. 1819.

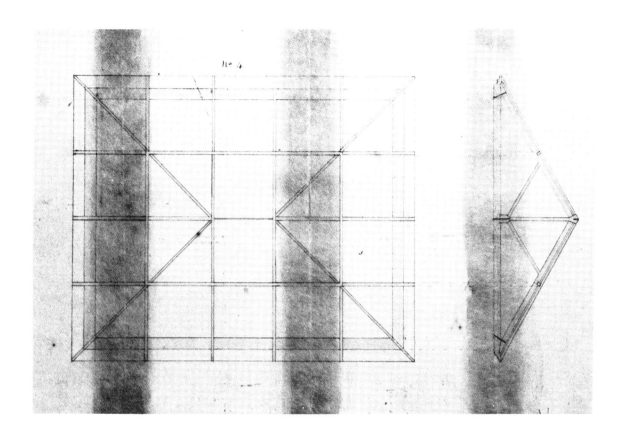

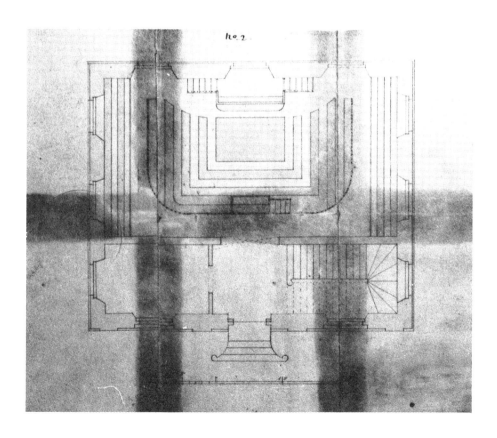

3 Beaufort Courthouse plans attributed to William Jay, c. 1819.

Plan 4

4 Courthouse elevation attributed to William Jay, c. 1820, and probably from a set of his stock plans.

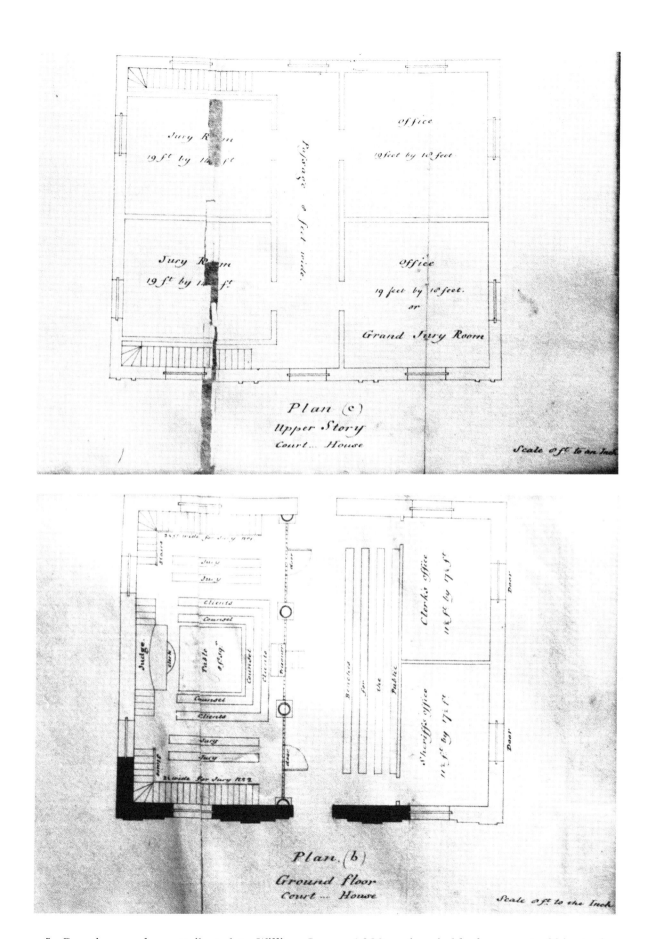

Plan (c)
Upper Story
Court... House

Jury Room
19 f.t by 14 f.t

Jury Room
19 f.t by 14 f.t

Office
19 feet by 18 feet

Office
19 feet by 18 feet
or
Grand Jury Room

Scale 6 f.t to an Inch

Plan (b)
Ground floor
Court ... House

Clerks office
14 f.t by 19 f.t

Sheriffs office
14 f.t by 19 f.t

Benches for the Public

Judge.

Table of Reg.r

Counsel

Clients

Jury

Counsel

Clients

Jury

Scale 6 f.t to the Inch

5 Courthouse plans attributed to William Jay, c. 1820, and probably from a set of his stock plans.

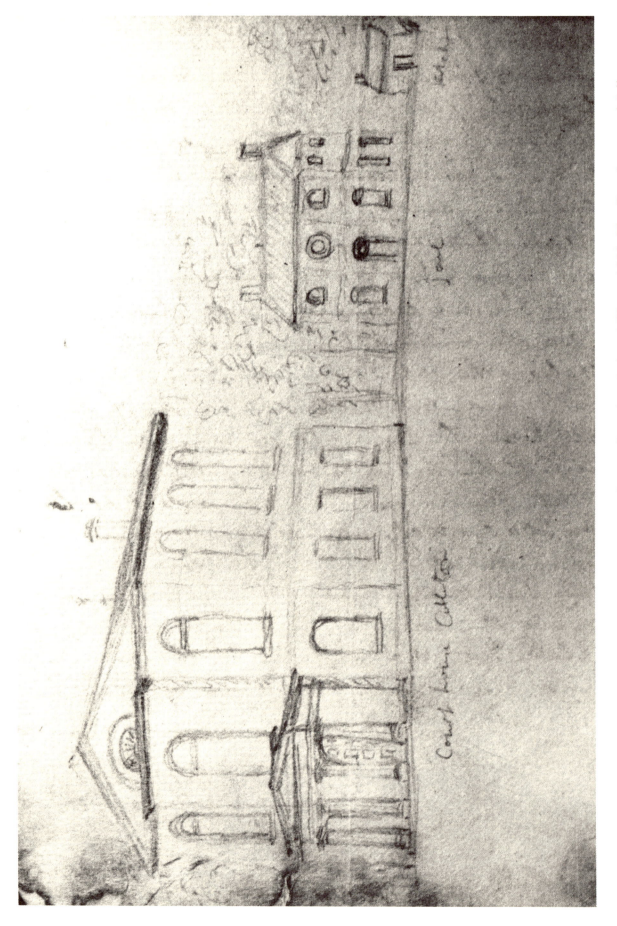

Court house Colleton

Jail

6 "Court house Colleton," "jail," and "kitchen;" drawing attributed to Robert Mills, c. 1822. The Courthouse and Jail were designed by Jay, but were redesigned by Mills.

7 "View of New and Old Court House, Winnsboro," drawn by Robert Mills, c. 1822. The new Fairfield District Courthouse (left) was designed by Jay in 1820 and redesigned by Mills in 1821.

8 (A) Newburyport, Massachusetts, Custom House by Robert Mills, 1833-1835. (B) Fairfield Courthouse as redesigned in c. 1844 and 1939 (photographed 1980).

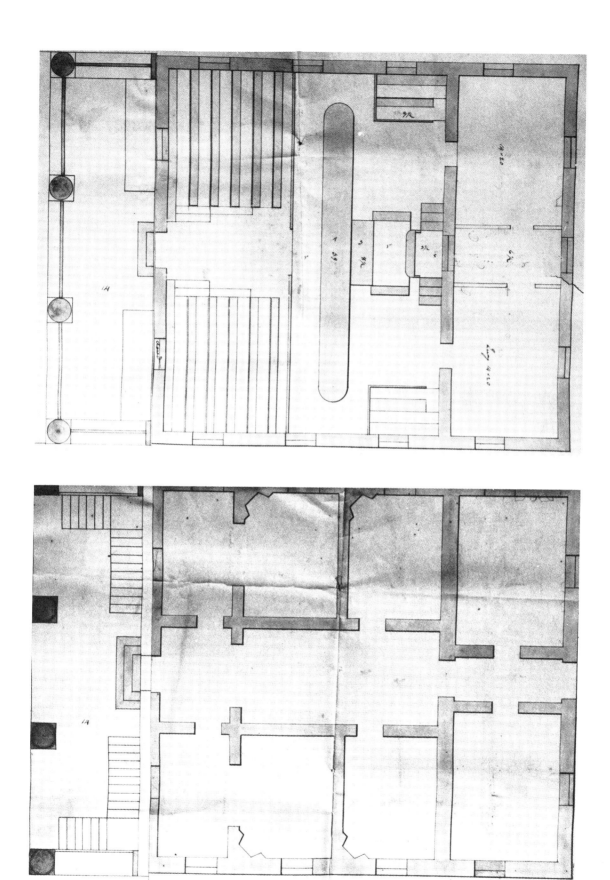

9 Fairfield Courthouse plans with the portico added to the front and rooms added to the back in c. 1844 (giving the building a greater depth than width).

10 (A) Sumter Courthouse by William Jay, built 1820-1821 and redesigned in 1839-1840. (B) Sumter Courthouse with further redesign.

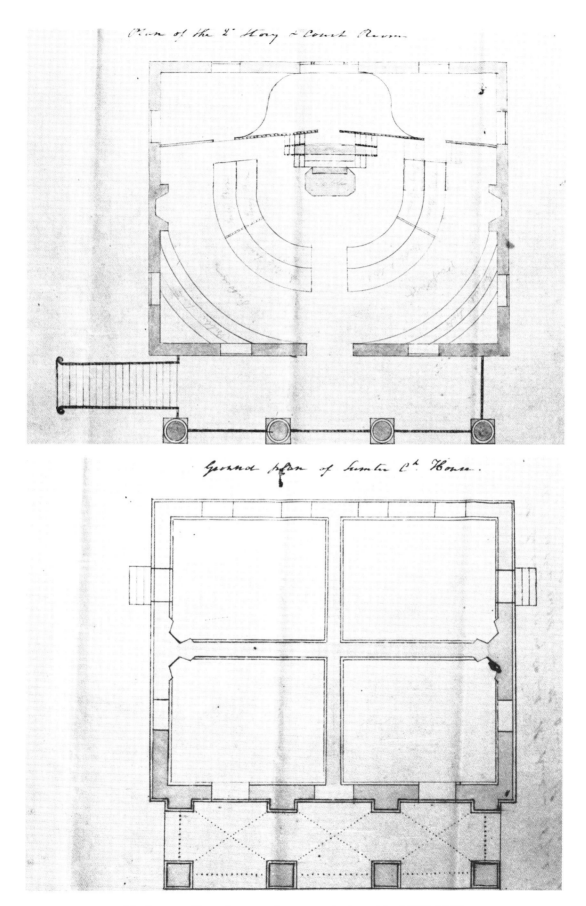

11 Sumter Courthouse plans as redesigned in 1839-1840.

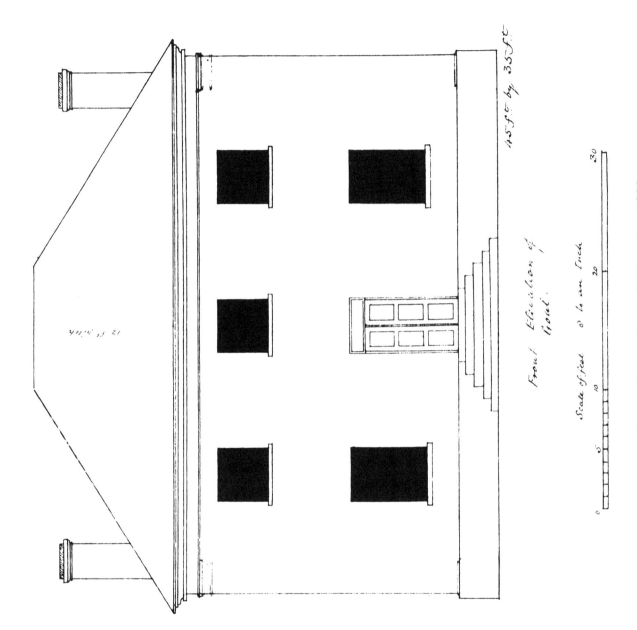

12 Pendleton jail elevation by William Jay, 1820.

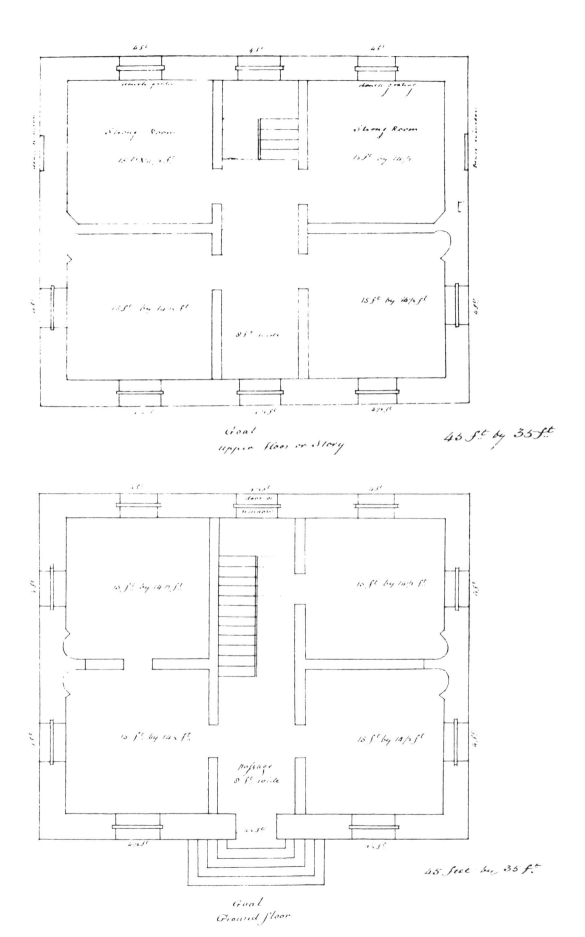

13 Pendleton Jail plans by William Jay, 1820.

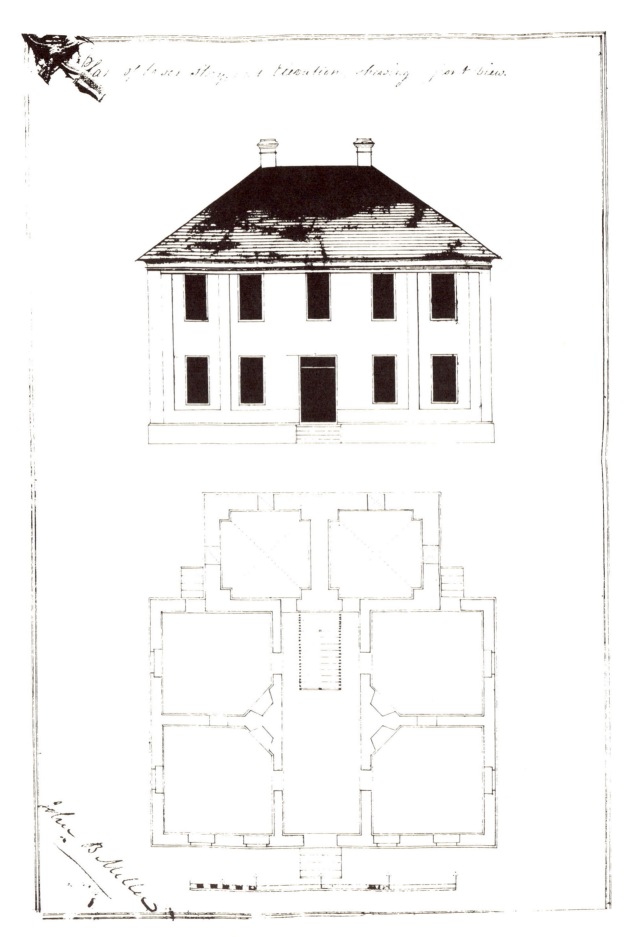

14 Sumter Jail elevation and plan, c. 1826. Influenced by Jay.

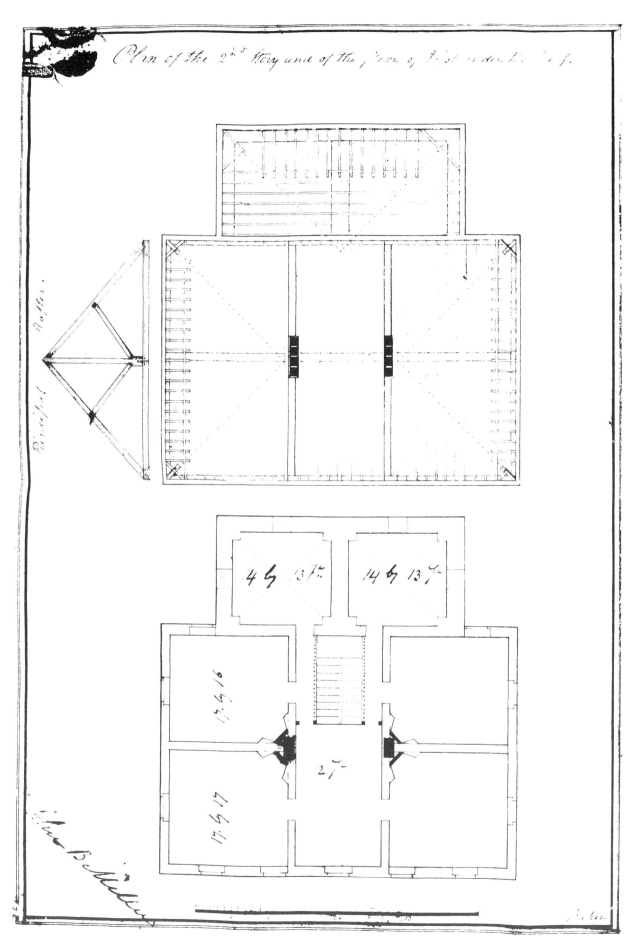

15 Sumter Jail plans, c. 1826.

16 "South East View of Greenville, South Carolina" by Joshua Tucker, 1825. Courthouse designed by Mills, c. 1821.

17 Greenville Courthouse as renovated (demolished 1924).

18 (A) Greenville Courthouse as renovated (rear view). (B) York Courthouse, designed by Mills in c. 1821 (1889 wood engraving).

19 (A) Villa Arsiero, Vicenza, attributed by Scamozzi to Palladio; 16th Century. (B) Orangeburg Courthouse, designed by Mills in c. 1825 (1865 wood engraving).

20 Union Courthouse, designed by Mills in c. 1821.

21 Horry Courthouse, designed by Mills in c. 1823.

22 Williamsburg Courthouse, designed by Mills in c. 1821 (upper story rebuilt c. 1883; photographed in 1951).

23 Georgetown Courthouse, designed by Mills in c. 1822 (rear addition added c. 1854).

24 (A) Pavilion VII, University of Virginia, designed by Thomas Jefferson (with the facade adapted from an elevation by William Thornton, 1817). (B) Chester Courthouse, designed by E.B. White, c. 1852.

25 (A) Kershaw Courthouse, as redesigned and enlarged in c. 1845 (designed by Mills in c. 1825 with six Ionic columns). (B) Virginia Capitol, Richmond, in c. 1790 (based on c. 1785 designs by Thomas Jefferson).

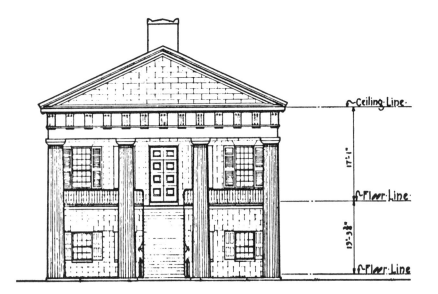

Ceiling Line

17'-1"

Floor Line

13'-3½"

Floor Line

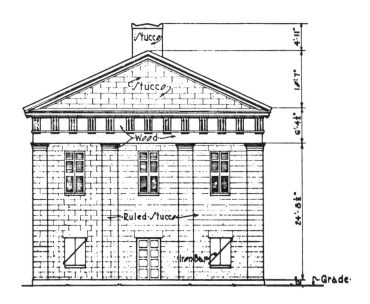

4'-11"

Stucco

Stucco

16'-7"

Wood

6'-4½"

Ruled Stucco

24'-0½"

Iron Bars

Grade

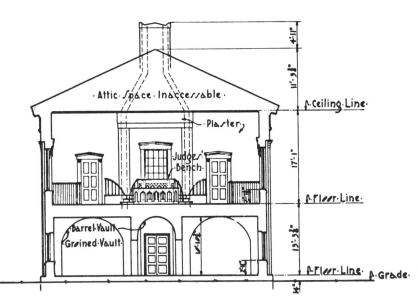

4'-11"

11'-3½"

Ceiling Line

Attic Space Inaccessable

Plaster

Judges Bench

17'-1"

Floor Line

Barrel Vault

Groined Vault

13'-3½"

Floor Line   Grade

26-27 Historic American Building Survey drawings of the Kershaw Courthouse, 1934.

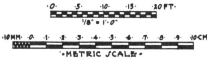

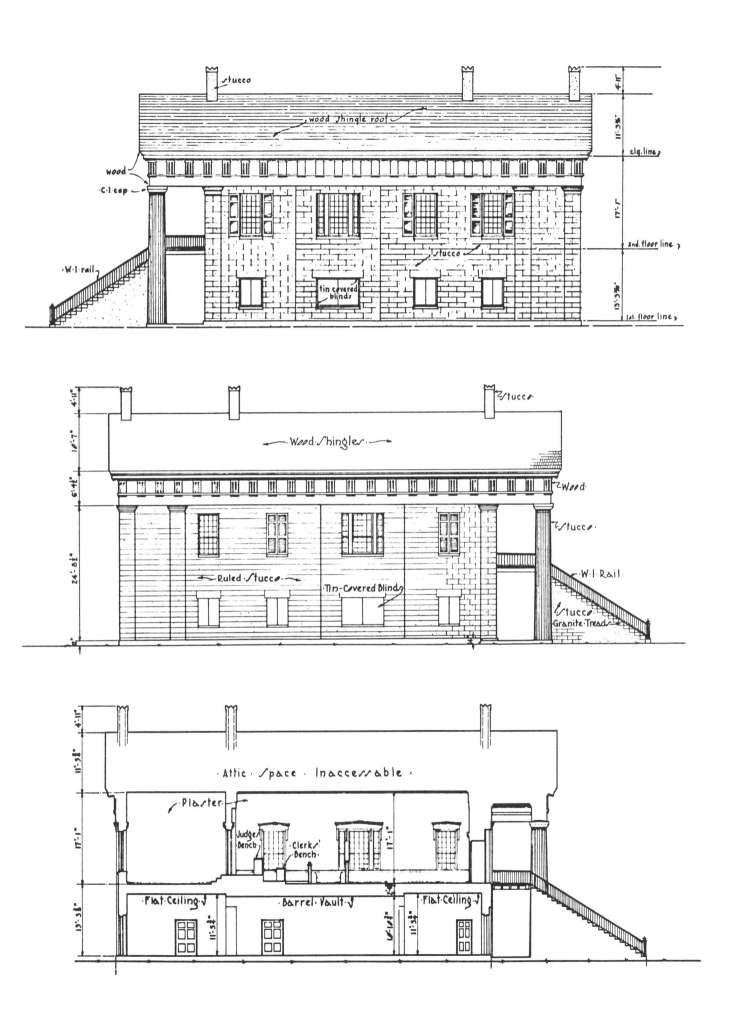

stucco

wood shingle roof

wood

C·l cap

·W·I·rail

stucco

tin covered blinds

4'-11"

11'-3⅜"

clg. line

17'-1"

2nd. floor line

13'-3⅜"

1st. floor line

Stucco

Wood Shingles

Wood

Stucco

W·I·Rail

Stucco
Granite Tread

Ruled Stucco

Tin-Covered Blinds

4'-11"

10'-7"

6'-4¼"

24'-8½"

2"

Attic Space Inaccessable

Plaster

Judges Bench

Clerks Bench

Flat Ceiling

Barrel Vault

Flat Ceiling

4'-11"

11'-5⅜"

17'-1"

11'-1"

13'-5⅜"

11'-5¼"

11'-10¾"

11'-5¼"

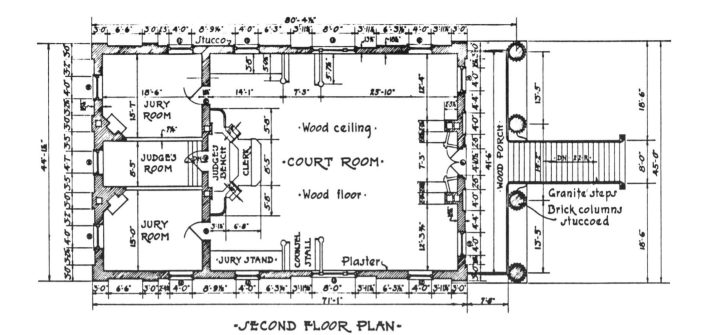

·SECOND FLOOR PLAN·

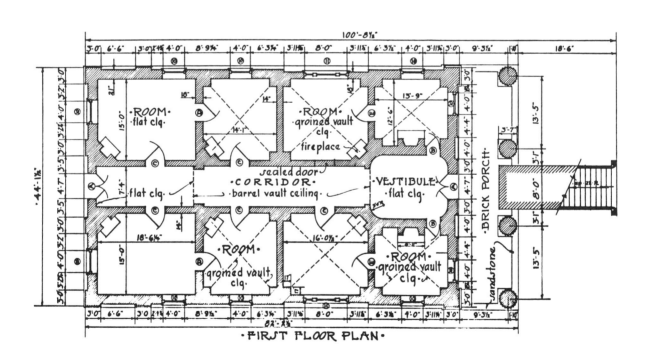

·FIRST FLOOR PLAN·

28 HABS drawings of the Kershaw Courthouse, 1934.

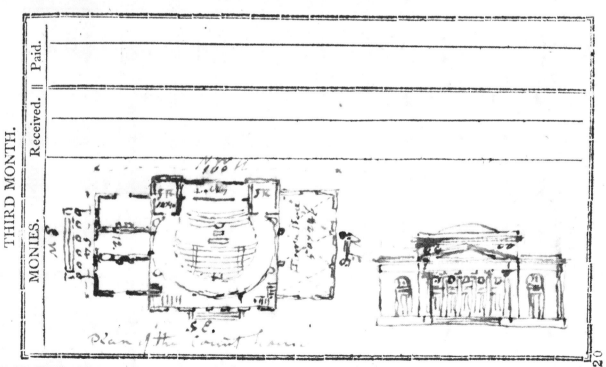

29 (A) Chesterfield Courthouse, designed by Mills, c. 1824 (1865 wood engraving). (B) Proposal for the Richmond City Hall and Courthouse by Mills, 1816.

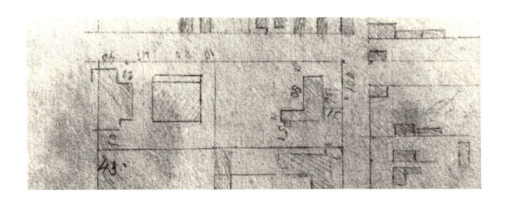

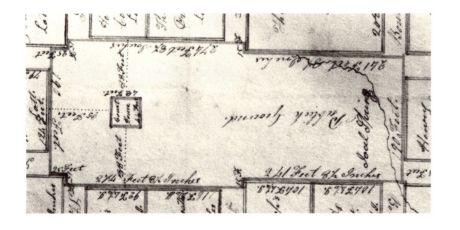

30 (A) Newberry Courthouse site, 1823. (B) Charleston Jail with Mills's c. 1821 wing (1851 plan). (C) Anderson Court-house and Jail of c. 1826 showing Mills's influence (1827 plan).

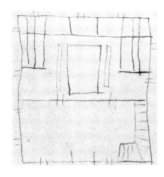
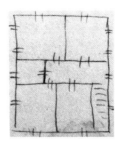

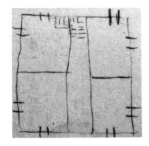

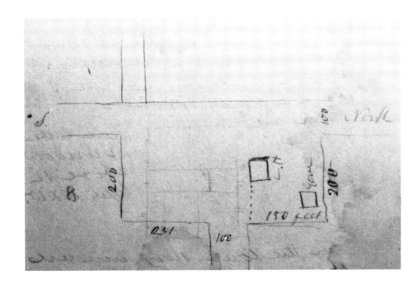

31 Darlington public buildings of c. 1803 - c. 1807 (drawn in 1822): (A-B) Courthouse, upper and lower floors. (C-D) Jail, upper and lower floors. (E) Town square.

32 Darlington Courthouse: (A) Building constructed 1824-1826 and attributed to Mills; rebuilt c. 1870 (photographed in c. 1880). (B) Addition at the back to match existing conditions in c. 1854.

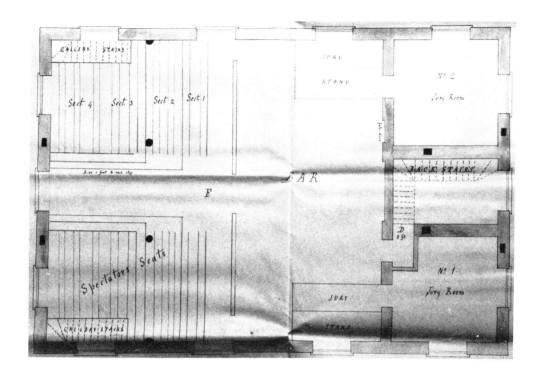

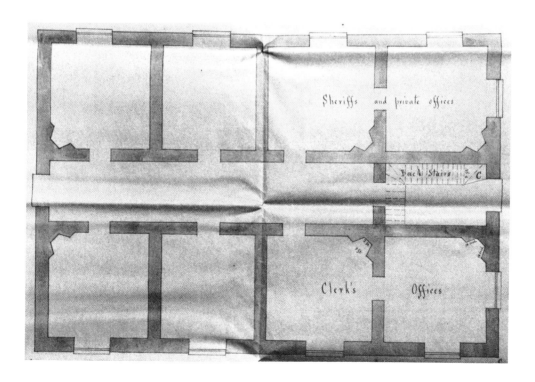

33 Darlington Courthouse renovation plans, c. 1854.

34 Union Jail, designed by Mills, c. 1821.

35 (A) Villa Saraceno by Andrea Palladio (note the horizontal windows and triple-arched, recessed porch). (B) Detail, Union Jail. (C) Union Jail.

36 (A) Spartanburg Jail, attributed to Mills and designed c. 1822 (destroyed c. 1913). (B) Lancaster Jail (photographed 1978).

Elevation of the Officers quarter facing the Yard

Elevation of the front of Commandants' quarters to the East

37   Elevations for the Officers' and Commandant's Quarters, Allagheny Arsenal, Pittsburgh, by Benjamin Henry Latrobe, 1814.

38 Lancaster Jail (photographed c. 1941).

39 Elevation of the Lunatic Asylum, Columbia; designed by Mills in c. 1821 (drawing, c. 1828).

40 Elevation of the Fireproof Building, Charleston; designed by Mills in c. 1821 (drawn in c. 1828).

41 Fireproof Building in 1883 (before damage by the earthquake of 1886).

42 Cross vaulting with corner supports in the Fireproof Building.

43 (A) Randolph Hall, College of Charleston; one of a pair of stairs for a portico on an arcaded base by E.B. White, c. 1850. (B) Asylum stairs as built (see **Figure 39**).

44 Bethesda Presbyterian Church, Camden; designed by Mills and completed in 1822. Engraved in 1827 after a drawing by Mills.

45 Columbia Female Academy; attributed to Mills. Lithograph of 1841 (compare **Figure** 29A).

46 Robert Mills House, Columbia; designed for Ainsley Hall by Mills in c. 1823.

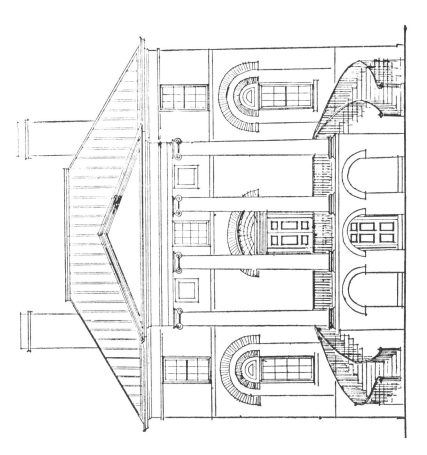

47 (A) Stair restoration proposed by Albert Simons, F.A.I.A., for the Robert Mills House, 1963. (B) Thomas Pinckney, Jr. House, Charleston; completed c. 1829 and redesigned or influenced by Mills.

FAÇADE of THE COURT - HOUSE for ALEXANDRIA.

48 Elevation for a courthouse at Alexandria, Virginia, by Mills, 1838.

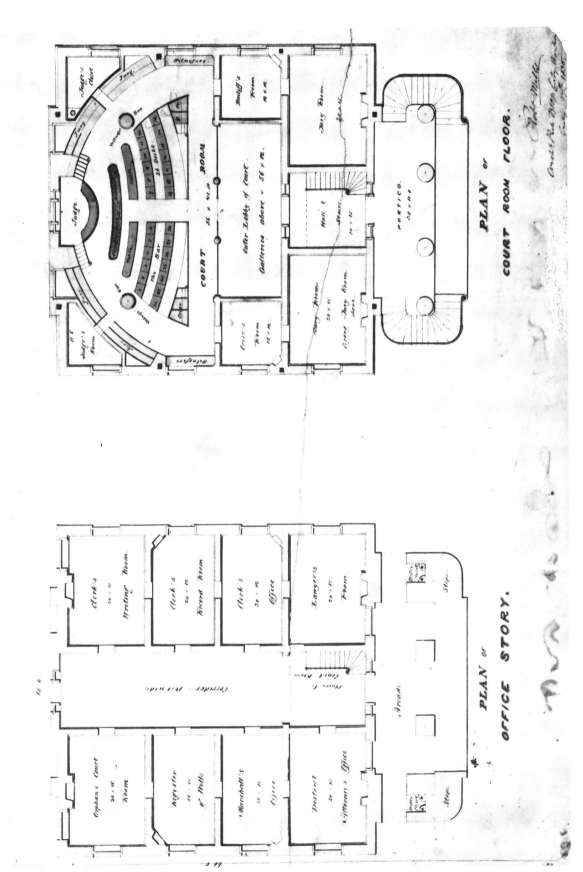

49 Plans for a courthouse at Alexandria, Virginia.

50 City Hall (c. 1800), Charleston, with the Charleston Courthouse to its left and the Fireproof Building to its right (photographed in 1886).

51 (A) Charleston Courthouse (rebuilt 1788-1797; photographed in 1883). (B) State House, Columbia (designed in c. 1786; watercolor by John Drayton painted in 1794).

52 (A) Lancaster Courthouse; attributed to W.W. Alsobrook, c. 1825 (photographed c. 1941). (B) Colleton Courthouse as rebuilt in 1842-1843 (photographed in c. 1900).

53 (A) Market Hall, Charleston, designed by E.B. White, c. 1841 (photographed in 1868). (B) Barnwell Courthouse, constructed in 1878-1879.

54 Edgefield Courthouse, built 1838-1839 (photographed in 1950).

55 (A) Marion Courthouse, designed c. 1851. (B) Cheraw Town Hall, built 1859.

56   (A) Abbeville Courthouse, designed c. 1852. (B) Cokesbury Female Seminary, Greenwood County, built c. 1841.

57 Aiken Courthouse: (A) As designed by R.W. McGrath, c. 1881. (B) As redesigned by Willis Irvin, 1934.

58 (A) Lance Hall, Circular Congregational Church, Charleston, built 1867. (B) The Richland Courthouse from 1872-1935.

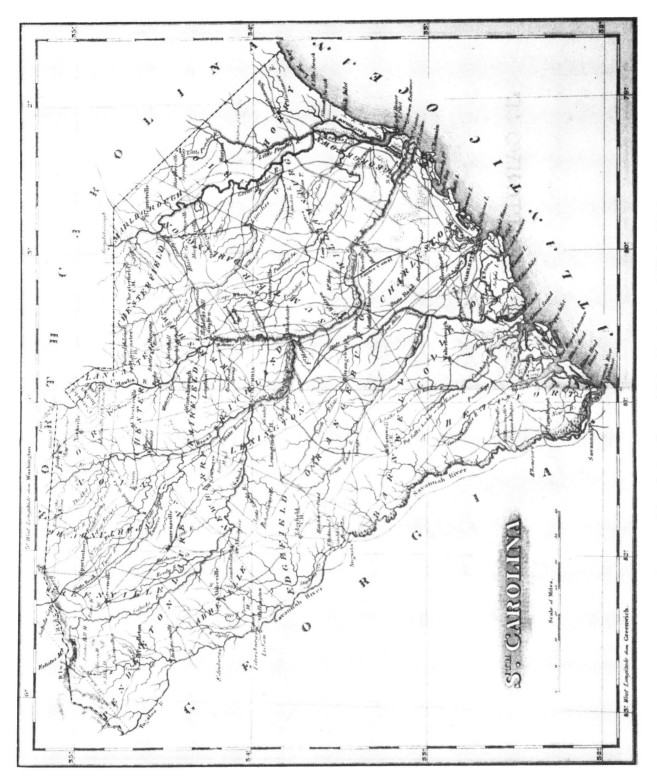

59 Map of South Carolina published by Robert Mills in 1825.

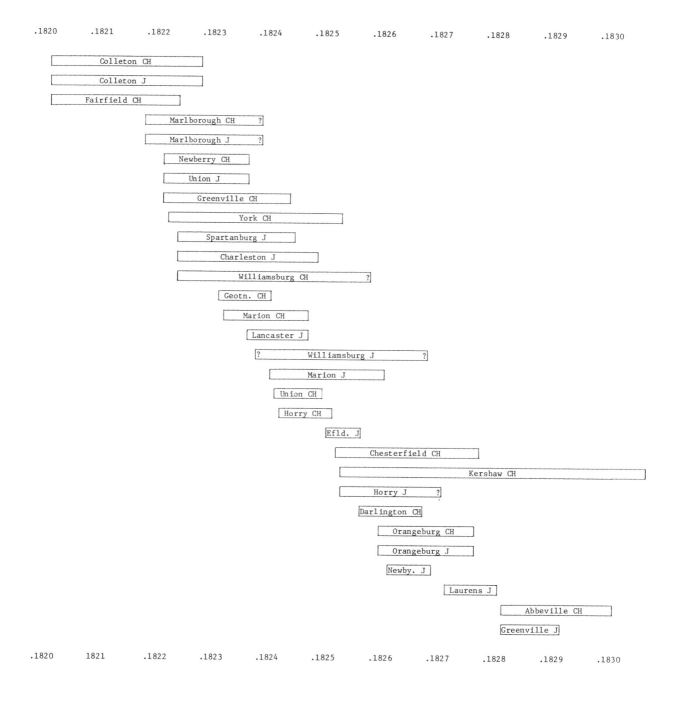

60 Graph with dates of construction for Mills's South Carolina courthouses and jails. The beginning and ending dates for construction are based largely on payment records of the State Treasurers (SCDAH). The length of time required for completion varied according to the complexity of Mills's design, the weather, delays in payment, the availability and suitability of materials, the amount of redesign, the competence and honesty of contractors, and the prompt receipt of the completed work by an authorized agent.

INDEX